DATE DUE

AP 24 '89			
OC 13 '89			
JE 8 '91			
NO 02 '01			
SE 11 02			

ARAB-ISRAELI CONFLICT

MODERN WORLD PROBLEMS

greenhaven press, inc.
577 Shoreview Park Road, St. Paul, Minnesota 55112

The Modern World Problems series was developed by the British Schools Council which was established by the British Department of Education and Science in cooperation with teacher organizations to develop innovative materials for the teaching of history. Greenhaven Press is pleased to offer this outstanding book series to American teachers and librarians for the study of world issues and social conflicts. The series is published in Great Britain by Holmes McDougall Ltd.

Project Team

David Sylvester *(Director to 1975)*
Tony Boddington *(Director 1975-1977)*
Gwenifer Griffiths (1975-1976)
William Harrison *(1972-1975)*
John Mann *(1974-1975)*
Aileen Plummer *(1972-1977)*
Denis Shemilt *(Evaluator 1974-1977)*
Peter Wenham *(to 1974)*

Design by George Nicol/Forth Studios
Picture research by Procaudio Limited

ISBN 0-912616-67-9 Paper Edition
ISBN 0-912616-68-7 Library Edition

CONTENTS

INTRODUCTION

What are your first reactions when you hear people talk about the Middle East today? Possibly dismay at the way people are continually fighting there; possibly fear that a third World War could start. Probably you also realise that this is the area we depend upon most for our precious supplies of oil. So the Middle East is vitally important to us today.

An oil refinery in the Persian Gulf

THE MIDDLE EAST

There is no universally accepted definition of the territory of the Middle East, but the limits of the area are usually shown to extend from Egypt in the west to the valleys of the Tigris and Euphrates in the east and from Turkey in the north to the Indian Ocean in the south (see Map).

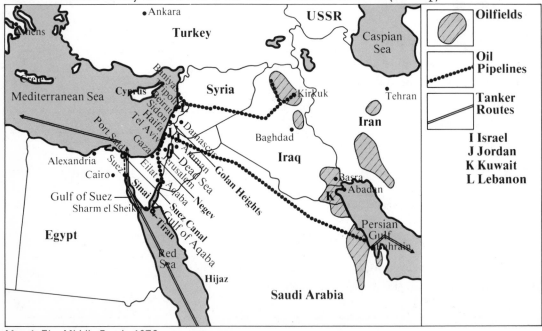

Map 1: The Middle East in 1976

Although the term 'Middle East' was first coined as recently as 1902 by the American naval historian A. T. Mahan, the region has been one of the most significant throughout world history. In the fertile river valleys of the Nile, the Tigris and the Euphrates the earliest civilisations developed. The Middle East is the source of three of the great religions of the world—Judaism, Christianity and Islam. It is here that Moses, Christ and Mohammed lived and taught. Great Empires have risen and fallen in the Middle East—for example the Ancient Empire of Egypt, the Arab Empire of the early middle ages and the Turkish Empire of modern times. Military leaders like Alexander, Julius Caesar and Napoleon have sought fame and conquest in this area.

The Middle East has been at the crossroads of power and trade. It is the meeting place of three continents. It has provided the setting for many fierce military, political, religious and commercial disputes throughout history.

THE PROBLEM OF PALESTINE

The Middle East in this century has been the focus of deep and bitter conflict between Jews and Arabs. Both claim the right to control and live in the small territory traditionally known as Palestine.

The problem is that both Jews and Arabs have strong claims to Palestine. According to tradition they have a common ancestor, Abraham. From Abraham's son Isaac came the Jewish race; from his other son Ishmael came the Arabs.

THE JEWISH CLAIM

The Old Testament is the story of the struggles of the Israelites (Jews) for survival, and their longing for their 'promised land' in Palestine, where they eventually settled about 1200 BC. In the first century AD, however, their troubles began once more. In 70 AD, after a revolt against the Romans, their Temple in Jerusalem was burnt. In 135 AD, after a second revolt, they were forbidden to assemble for prayer or visit Jerusalem, their holy city, again. For the next eighteen centuries they were a people without a homeland, dispersed throughout the world. But they never lost their identity and pride as Jews nor their aim of returning one day to Palestine and their holy city, Jerusalem.

Jews and Arabs demonstrate outside the Israeli Embassy, December 1973

THE ARAB CLAIM

In the seventh century AD, Palestine was taken over by the Arabs as they spread the Islamic religion through the Middle East and North Africa. During this period they built many religious shrines in Palestine, and Jerusalem also became for them a sacred place.

At the beginning of this century Arab peoples were still living in Palestine. But the Jews, too, became increasingly determined to reclaim Palestine as their homeland. In 1948, after the Second World War, a Jewish State was finally established in Palestine. The Jews once more had a country of their own which they renamed Israel. But this was also the homeland of Arab peoples. The Arabs felt that the land had been taken from them without any justification and they were determined to fight for it. This, in brief, is the root of the Arab-Israeli Conflict.

THE ARAB-ISRAELI CONFLICT

Since 1948 there have been four wars in the Middle East, all focussing on this land, disputed by the Arabs and Israelis. So far, except in 1956, other countries have not joined in directly. The Americans and the Russians supply arms and other countries, particularly Britain and France, are very concerned about what happens in the Middle East. We shall be trying to find out why they are so concerned and how much influence other individual countries and the United Nations have over the Arabs and Israelis. But first we must trace what has happened in the Middle East in recent years. The story is often complicated, but it is exciting and important. People are fighting for what they believe to be the highest ideals, but in doing so they are causing other people to starve and threatening the peace of the world.

This book is divided into two parts: the first outlines the conflict from the beginnings of the Zionist movement to establish a national homeland for the Jews to the present day; the second provides a short discussion of some of the present major issues.

An Egyptian attack on an Israeli position in the 1973 war

PART 1
1 THE ORIGINS OF THE CONFLICT

At the end of the nineteenth century the Turks still ruled much of the Middle East, but three things were happening:

(i) European countries were becoming more involved in the area;

(ii) the Arabs were trying to gain freedom from Turkish rule;

(iii) European and American Jews were beginning to work to establish a Jewish national home in Palestine.

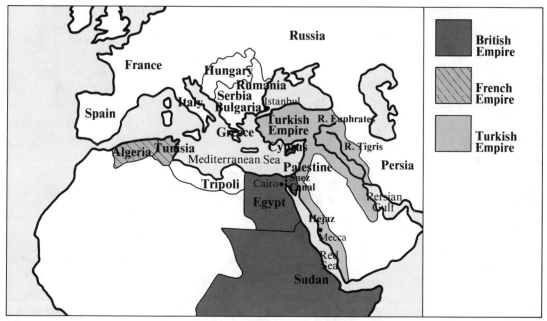

Map 2: The Middle East and the Turkish Empire in 1900

The opening ceremony of the Suez Canal at Port Said in 1869

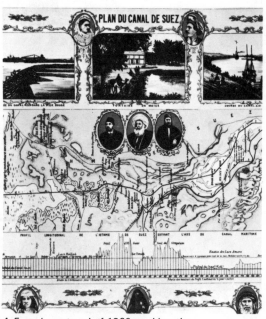

A French postcard of 1869 marking the opening of the Suez Canal

7

THE INVOLVEMENT OF EUROPEAN COUNTRIES

By 1900 Britain and France had established footholds in various areas of the Middle East.

In 1869 the Suez Canal was opened. British statesmen soon realised that influence over the administration of the canal—soon to be called the 'richest ditch in the world'—was of great importance. The canal which linked the Mediterranean Sea with the Indian Ocean was a quick route for trade and communications with the Far East and the Indian Empire. Accordingly, in 1876 the British Prime Minister, Disraeli, purchased 44 per cent of the Canal Company's stock from Egypt's bankrupt ruler. In 1882 British forces put down an Egyptian revolt and the British occupied Egypt. British rule was extended further south over the Sudan by the victory of General Kitchener's army at Omdurman in 1898.

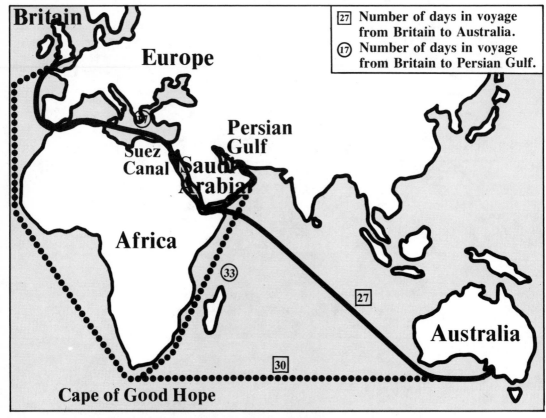

Map 3: The advantages of the Suez Canal

The Lion's Share: a Punch *cartoon of 26 February 1876*

The French also had interests in the Middle East—or Near East, as they called it. French merchants had been active in Syria for a long time, and Algeria and Tunisia were part of the French Empire. Moreover, a Frenchman, Ferdinand de Lesseps, had designed and built the Suez Canal, and a proportion of the Suez Canal Company stock was held by the French.

By 1900 it was clear to statesmen in Europe that before long the Turkish (or Ottoman) Empire would collapse. The European countries, Italy and Germany as well as Britain and France, hoped to gain from this and establish greater influence in the Middle East. They were becoming more interested in the newly found oil of Persia.

AN ARAB MOVEMENT TO GAIN FREEDOM FROM TURKISH RULE

From the 1880s onwards there were various movements amongst the Arabs to remove their Turkish overlords and establish Arab rule in the Middle East, including Palestine. One was called the League of Arab Fatherland, and in 1905 a Christian Arab in Paris, Negib Azouri, outlined the aim of the League:

The League wants, before everything else ... to form an Arab Empire stretching from the Tigris and the Euphrates to the Suez Isthmus, and from the Mediterranean to the Arabian Sea.

Although the Arabs were by no means united, they shared much in common. Most Arabs were of the Muslim or Islamic religion. This religion had been established by the teachings of the Prophet Mohammed in Arabia during the seventh century and became one of the greatest of the world's religions. Also, many Arabs recalled the memory of their great days in the middle ages when an Arab Empire extended from the Pyrénees in Spain to the plains of India. During this period the Arabs were famed as doctors, scientists, mathematicians and craftsmen. The unity of the Arab people was expressed in the Arabic language. For centuries it had been the common language of the Muslim world, whether in the classical form of the Holy Book, the Koran, or in the various regional forms.

Many Arabs became aware of the success of peoples in Europe, like the Italians and Germans, who had formed their own nation states in the nineteenth century. They began to seek a similar independence from their Ottoman rulers, in spite of the fact that the Turks followed the same Muslim religion. Although there were some influential Arabs in Europe campaigning for independence, the main source of leadership in the Middle East lay in the Hejaz area with Sherif Hussein of Mecca and his two sons, Abdullah and Feisal.

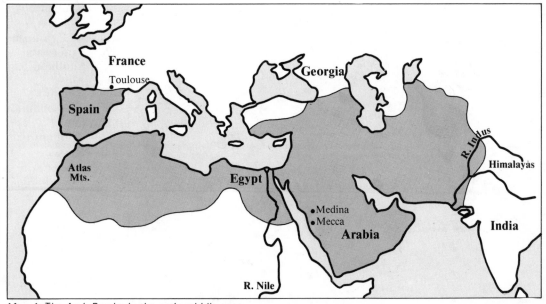

Map 4: The Arab Empire in the early middle ages

9

The Arab Nationalist Manifesto

The movement gathered strength and in 1914 a manifesto of Arab nationalism was issued from Cairo. It gives you some idea of the kind of appeal which the leaders made:

Source 1

O Arabs . . . how long will you remain asleep? . . . Do you not know that you live in a period when he who sleeps dies, and he who dies is gone forever? When will you know that your country has been sold to the foreigner? . . . The country is yours, and they say that rule belongs to the people, but those who exercise rule over you . . . inflict on you all kinds of suffering, tyranny and persecution. In their eyes you are but a flock of sheep whose wool is to be clipped, whose milk is to be drunk and whose meat is to be eaten . . .

Has your Arab blood congealed in your veins, and has it changed into dirty water? You have become, by God, a byword among the nations, a laughing stock of the world, a subject of mockery and derision among the peoples. You have almost become proverbial in your humility, weakness and acquiescence in great loss.

. . . Arise, O ye Arabs! Unsheathe the sword from the scabbard. Do not let an oppressive tyrant who has only disdain for you remain in your country; cleanse your country from those who show their enmity to you, to your race and to your language.

O ye Arabs! . . . You all dwell in one land, you speak one language, so be also one nation and one land.

Do not become divided against yourselves according to the designs and purposes of the troublemakers who feign Islam, while Islam is really innocent of their misdeeds.

(from S. Haim,
Arab Nationalism,
University of California Press, 1962,
pp. 83–88)

But although many Arabs believed in unity, they were not agreed on how to overthrow their Turkish rulers.

Map 5: The history of the Jewish people from 70 A.D.

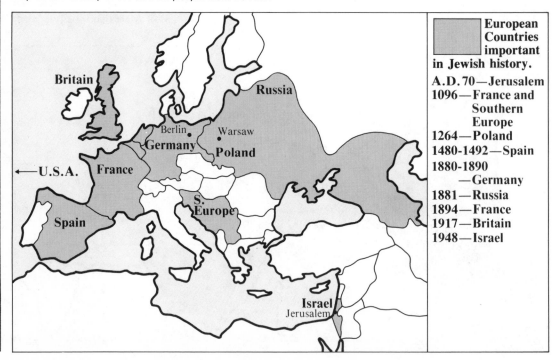

European Countries important in Jewish history.

A.D. 70—Jerusalem
1096—France and Southern Europe
1264—Poland
1480-1492—Spain
1880-1890 —Germany
1881—Russia
1894—France
1917—Britain
1948—Israel

ZIONISM: A MOVEMENT TO ESTABLISH A JEWISH NATIONAL HOME IN PALESTINE

At the same time as the Arabs were seeking freedom from Turkish rule, a movement led by European Jews was established to set up a Jewish home in Palestine.

The dispersion of the Jews

The Jewish state in Palestine collapsed in 70 AD after a revolt against the Romans. The Jewish Temple in Jerusalem, the focus of their religion and way of life, was destroyed. After a second revolt in 135 AD they were forbidden to visit Jerusalem again. The people who survived this revolt were scattered in all directions. Some migrated to other areas of the Middle East. Others journeyed to Europe—to Spain, Greece, Italy and France.

For nineteen centuries the Jews had no national homeland. Many, strengthened by their faith, continued to hope and pray for a return to Zion (Jerusalem). The Day of Atonement, concluded with a prayer expressing the hope of 'The Next Year in Jerusalem'.

Persecution of the Jews

During the centuries of dispersion many Jewish communities in European countries suffered persecution. The first attacks on Jews were made in 1096 in France and the Rhineland by Crusaders bound for the Holy Land. Later in Spain the Inquisition persecuted the Jews and between 1480 and 1492 thousands died at the stake. Many Jews moved east but in 1881 pogroms broke out in the Ukraine in Russia.

Between 1881 and 1914 three million Jews fled from eastern Europe because of the persecution they had suffered there. Some went to Palestine, but over one and a half million went to America. There were other anti-semitic movements in Germany and France. For example, in 1894 there was the notorious Dreyfus affair. Dreyfus, a Jewish officer in the French army, was accused of giving military secrets to Germany and he was used as a scapegoat, to cover the crimes of others.

Many reasons have been suggested for the long history of persecution of the Jews. First it may be seen as a reaction against the Jewish belief that they are a 'Chosen People'. Secondly, the Jews have been accused of being responsible for the crucifixion of Jesus Christ. Third, in the middle ages, the Roman Catholic Church forbade Christians to be money-lenders. Many Jews found that this unpopular role was forced upon them as they were frequently barred from other professions. Fourthly, because of their religion and minority position Jews have frequently been used as scapegoats for every kind of short-coming in the countries in which they lived.

An attack on a Jew in Kiev, Russia, in the late nineteenth century

Theodor Herzl, founder of Zionism

The renewal of persecution in the late nineteenth century caused many Jews to doubt whether they could continue to live in certain countries in Europe. A movement developed in the 1880s to establish a Jewish National Home. Theodor Herzl (1861–1904) was the founder of Zionism. His book *The Jewish State* was published in 1896. In it he outlined the aims of the movement:

Source 2

I shall content myself with putting the following questions to the Jews: Is it not true that in countries where we live in perceptible numbers, the position of Jewish lawyers, doctors, technicians, teachers and employees of all descriptions become daily more intolerable? Is it not true that the Jewish middle classes are seriously threatened? Is it not true that the passions of the mob are incited against our wealthy people? Is it not true that our poor endure greater sufferings than any other proletariat?

Everything tends in fact to one and the same conclusion, which is clearly enunciated in that classic Berlin phrase: 'Juden raus!' [out with the Jews].

I shall now put the question in the briefest possible form: Are we to get out now, and where to?

Or may we remain, and how long?

Let us first settle the point of staying where we are. Can we hope for better days? I say we cannot hope for a change in the current of feeling. And why not? Even if we were as near to the hearts of princes as are their other subjects, they could not protect us. They would only feed popular hatred by showing us too much favour.

He described his plan as 'perfectly simple': the Jews were to be granted 'a portion of the globe large enough to satisfy the rightful requirements of a nation'.

We must not imagine the departure of the Jews to be a sudden one. It will be gradual, continuous and will cover many decades. The poorest will go first to cultivate the soil. In accordance with a preconceived plan they will construct roads, bridges, railways and telegraph installations, regulate rivers, and build their own dwellings; their labour will create trade, trade will create markets and markets will attract new settlers. The emigrants standing lowest in the economic scale will be slowly followed by those of a higher grade. Those who at this moment are living in despair will go first.

The Basle Declaration

Theodor Herzl organised the first Zionist Congress, which was held in Switzerland in 1897. The Congress issued the following official statement, known as *The Basle Declaration*:

Source 3

The aim of Zionism is to create for the Jewish people a home in Palestine secured by public law.

The Congress contemplates the following means to the attainment of this end:

1. The promotion, on suitable lines, of the colonisation of Palestine by Jewish agricultural and industrial workers.

2. The organisation and binding together of the whole of Jewry by means of appropriate institutions, local and international, in accordance with the laws of each country.

3. The strengthening and fostering of Jewish national sentiment and consciousness.

4. Preparatory steps towards obtaining government consent, where necessary, to the attainment of the aim of Zionism.

   (from *The Israel-Arab Reader*, edited by W. Laqueur, Weidenfeld & Nicolson, 1969, pp. 11–12)

BIOGRAPHY: THEODOR HERZL

Theodor Herzl, an Austrian Jew, was the founder of political Zionism, the movement to establish a Jewish homeland in Palestine. While working as a journalist in Paris and Vienna in the 1880s and 1890s he faced much anti-semitism. This convinced him that the Jews would never be accepted into Western society and so they must organise a State of their own.

In 1896 he published a book called *The Jewish State* which argued his case. In the following year he founded the World Congress of Zionists and organised its first meeting in Basle, Switzerland. He became the first President of the World Zionist Organisation set up by the Congress. He established a Zionist weekly newspaper, *Die Welt*, in Vienna and entered into unsuccessful negotiations with Turkey and Britain for mass Jewish settlement in Palestine or Sinai.

In 1903 Herzl quarrelled with members of the Zionist Congress when he argued in support of a British offer of land for Jewish settlement in Uganda. His basic ideas about Zionism and programme of action lived on after his death in 1904 at the age of 44. His most significant achievement was that he had persuaded the then greatest power in the world, Great Britain, to take the Zionist cause seriously.

Chaim Weizmann, another Zionist leader, (right) and Lord Balfour (Centre) in Jerusalem, 1925

13

In Britain the Zionist movement grew mainly because of the work of Chaim Weizmann, who had come to England in 1904 as a bio-chemist at Manchester University. He interested influential people in Britain in the Zionist Movement, men like C. P. Scott, Editor of the *Manchester Guardian*, and Lloyd George and Arthur Balfour, famous politicians of the time.

2 THE IMPACT OF WAR

The outbreak of the First World War in 1914 proved a turning point in the destinies of both Arab and Jewish peoples.

In October 1914 Turkey entered the war on the side of Germany and Austria. The British became increasingly involved in diplomatic and military activity in the Middle East. During the war the British government made three undertakings concerning the Middle East: the first was with the Arabs; the second with France; and the third with the Zionist movement.

NEGOTIATIONS WITH THE ARABS

Previously the British had supported the Turkish Empire in order to check Russian influence in the Middle East and Asia. You can see from the map that if Russia gained a foothold in the Mediterranean she could be a danger to Britain's naval power and shipping routes. But now that Russia was fighting on the same side as Britain, and Turkey was the enemy, Britain was anxious to give every encouragement to the Arabs to rise up in revolt against their Turkish overlords. In return Britain would support Arab nationalism.

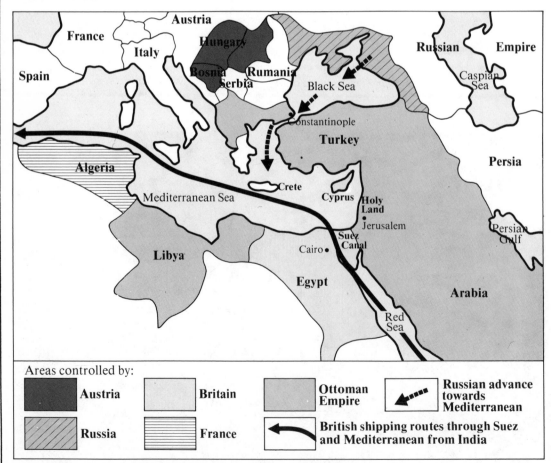

Map 6: The Mediterranean area in 1912, showing Russian ambitions

The Kitchener Letter

In November 1914 the following letter from Lord Kitchener, who had previously been British Consul-general in Egypt and was now Secretary of State for War, to Sherif Hussein began the negotiations.

Source 4

Till now we have defended and be-friended Islam in the person of the Turks. Henceforward it shall be that of the noble Arab. It may be that an Arab of true race will assume the caliphate at Mecca or Medina, and so good may come by the help of God out of all the evil which is now occurring. It would be well if your Highness could convey to your followers and devotees who are found throughout the world in every country the good tidings of the freedom of the Arabs and the rising of the sun over Arabia.

(Sykes papers. From E. Monroe, *Britain's Moment in the Middle East 1914–1956,* Chatto and Windus, 1963)

It is clear from this message that one of the ways in which the British hoped to draw Hussein into the war was by satisfying some of his personal ambitions. The Sherif was very anxious to take the office of Caliph—that is the civil and religious leader of all Muslims. Traditionally the Caliphate had been held by the Sultan of Turkey. Sherif Hussein believed that he had a far better right to this title as he claimed to be a descendant of the Prophet Mohammed while the Sultan was a member of the Turkish race rather than a true Arab.

Sherif Hussein's demands

During 1915–16 there was an exchange of letters between Hussein and the British High Commissioner for Egypt, Sir Henry McMahon. In the early stages the British promises tended to be vague and Sherif Hussein was anxious to secure specific terms.

BIOGRAPHY: SHERIF HUSSEIN OF MECCA

Sherif Hussein was born in Istanbul in 1854 and became one of the first Arab nationalist leaders. Even before World War I (1914–18) he was disillusioned by the treatment of the Arabs in the Turkish Empire. The outbreak of war in 1914 gave him the chance of enlisting the help of the British in the Arab fight for independence.

He was an important leader in the Arab revolt of 1916 against the Turks and he became King of Hejaz in the same year. However, he felt betrayed by the British when the Balfour Declaration was published, and was further angered by the setting up of the mandatory system in Syria, Palestine and Jordan after the war. Hussein felt that it denied the Arabs full independence. Meanwhile his relations with another great Arab leader, Ibn Saud, deteriorated. In 1924 Saud invaded the Hejaz and Hussein fled to Cyprus where he lived until just before his death in 1931.

In a letter dated the 14th of July 1915 he set out certain demands:

Source 5

Firstly—England to acknowledge the independence of the Arab countries, bounded on the north by Mersina and Adana up to the 37° latitude, on which degree fall Birijik, Urfa, Mardin, . . . Amadia, up to the border of Persia ; on the east by the borders of Persia up to the Gulf of Basra ; on the South by the Indian Ocean, with the exception of the position of Aden to remain as it is ; on the west by the Red Sea, the Mediterranean Sea up to Mersina. England to approve of the proclamation of an Arab Caliphate of Islam.

[Five other demands made by Sherif Hussein are omitted.]

(Official English translation of Document No. 1 from *The Correspondence between Sir Henry McMahon and Sherif Hussein of Mecca, July 1915–March 1916*, HMSO)

Sir Henry McMahon

British promises: the McMahon letter

The detailed promises which Britain eventually gave to Sherif Hussein are clearly set out in McMahon's letter. You can imagine what the Arabs regarded Britain's attitude towards them to be, after reading this letter:

Map 7: Sherif Hussein's demands

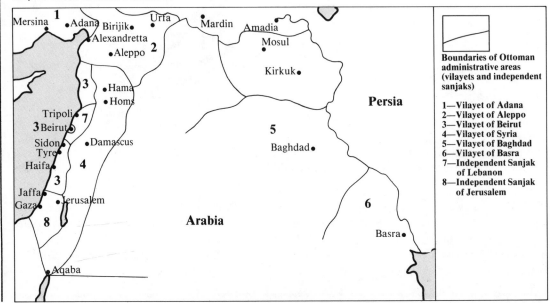

Boundaries of Ottoman administrative areas (vilayets and independent sanjaks)

1—Vilayet of Adana
2—Vilayet of Aleppo
3—Vilayet of Beirut
4—Vilayet of Syria
5—Vilayet of Baghdad
6—Vilayet of Basra
7—Independent Sanjak of Lebanon
8—Independent Sanjak of Jerusalem

(1) Subject to modifications, Great Britain is prepared to recognise and support the independence of the Arabs in all the regions within the limits demanded by the Sherif of Mecca.

(2) Great Britain will guarantee the Holy Places against all external aggression and will recognise their inviolability.

(3) When the situation admits, Great Britain will give to the Arabs her advice and will assist them to establish what may appear to be the most suitable forms of government in those various territories.

(4) On the other hand, it is understood that the Arabs have decided to seek the advice and guidance of Great Britain only, and that such European advisers and officials as may be required for the formation of a sound form of administration will be British.

(5) With regard to the vilayets of Baghdad and Basra, the Arabs will recognise that the established positions and interests of Great Britain necessitate special administrative arrangements in order to secure their territories from foreign aggression, to promote the welfare of the local population and to safeguard our mutual economic interests.

I am convinced that this declaration will assure you beyond all possible doubt of the sympathy of Great Britain towards the aspirations of her friends the Arabs and will result in a firm and lasting alliance, the immediate results of which will be the expulsion of the Turks from the Arab countries and the freeing of the Arab peoples from the Turkish yoke, which for so many years has pressed heavily upon them.

(from W. Laqueur, *The Israel-Arab Reader*)

Lawrence of Arabia and the Turkish revolt

Although the Sherif was not entirely satisfied with McMahon's assurances, the Arab revolt against the Turks began on 10 June 1916.

Prince Feisal, son of Sherif Hussein

BIOGRAPHY: T E LAWRENCE

T. E. Lawrence was an archeological scholar, military strategist and author. He is best known, however, for his legendary war activities as Lawrence of Arabia, which he described in his book *Seven Pillars of Wisdom*.

His interest in the Middle East began as a student at Oxford University and he travelled widely in the area before 1914. When war broke out in 1914 he joined the British Army and was sent to Cairo where he was given a post in the Intelligence Section. During a trip to Arabia, he became convinced that aid to the Arabs was the way to weaken Turkey, Germany's ally. With the help of a British diplomat who had accompanied him to Arabia, Lawrence persuaded Sherif Hussein's sons to let him command an Arab force in the rebellion against the Turks. Lawrence organised his Arab troops as a guerrilla force at first. Later, he tried to coordinate Arab movements with those of the British Army. But Lawrence became disillusioned by British policy. Under the Sykes-Picot agreement, Britain denied the Arabs the full independence they had been promised despite their victories over the Turks.

After the war Lawrence pressed in vain for Arab independence. He found it difficult to settle down to ordinary civilian life, and twice joined the services under assumed names. He also took up writing. He spent the last years of his life working on sea plane design for the RAF. He died in 1935 in a motor cycle accident, aged 46.

Feisal, Hussein's son, played a large part in this revolt. He was assisted by Colonel T. E. Lawrence—the legendary Lawrence of Arabia—whose account of the Arab campaigns in the desert appeared in his book *Seven Pillars of Wisdom*.

The Arab tribesmen succeeded in cutting off vital supplies and communications by harassing the Damascus-Medina railway and by swift guerrilla attacks on detachments of the Turkish Army. Here is Lawrence of Arabia's description of an attack on the Damascus-Medina Railway in 1917:

Source 7

From the southern bridge we brought the electric leads to the middle bridge, whose arch would conceal the exploder from a train overhead.

The Lewis guns we put under the Northern bridge, to rake the far side of the train when the mine went off. The Arabs would line the bushes of a cross-channel of the valley three hundred yards our side of the railway. We waited afterwards throughout a day of sunlight and flies. Enemy patrols marched actively along the line, morning, afternoon and evening.

On the second day, about eight in the morning, a pillar of smoke left Maan. With twelve loaded wagons the engine panted on the upgrade. I sat by a bush in the stream-bed, a hundred yards from the mine; in view of it and of the exploder-party and of the machine guns. When Faiz and Bedri heard the engine over their arch, they danced a war-dance round their little electric box. The Arabs in the ditch were hissing softly to me that it was time to fire; but not until the engine was exactly over the arch did I jump up and wave my cloak. Faiz instantly pressed his handle, and the great noise and dust and blackness burst up, and enveloped me where I sat, while the green-yellow sickly smoke of lyddite hung sluggishly about the wreck. The Lewis guns rattled out suddenly, three or four short bursts; there was a yell from the Arabs, and they rushed in a wild torrent for the train.

Our mine had taken out the near arch of the bridge. Of the locomotive, the fire-box was torn open, and many tubes burst. The cab was cleared out, a cylinder gone, the frame buckled, two driving wheels and their journals shattered. The tender and first waggon had telescoped. About twenty Turks were dead, and others prisoners, including four officers, who stood by the line weeping for the life which the Arabs had no mind to take.

The contents of the trucks were foodstuffs, some seventy tons of them; 'urgently needed', according to the way-bill, in Medain Salih. We sent one way-bill to Feisal, as detailed report of our success, and left the other receipted in the van. We also kicked northward some dozen civilians, who had thought they were going to Medina.

Farraj held my camel, while Salem and Dheilan helped with the exploder and the too-heavy wire. Rescue parties of Turks were four hundred yards away when we had finished, but we rode off without a man killed or wounded.

My pupils practised the art of mining afterwards by themselves and taught others.

In the next four months our experts from Akaba destroyed seventeen locomotives. Travelling became an uncertain terror for the enemy. At Damascus people scrambled for the back seats in trains, even paid extra for them. The engine-drivers struck. Civilian traffic nearly ceased. The loss of the engines was sore upon the Turks.

(from T. E. Lawrence, *Seven Pillars of Wisdom*, Penguin Books, 1961)

Wrecked railway trucks at Ghedir el Hej

In 1917 the British forces under General Allenby launched an attack from their bases in Egypt. Egypt had been declared a British Protectorate in December 1914 in view of its strategic importance. By October 1918 the Arab forces and the British army had driven the Turkish Army out of Arab lands. The Arabs now waited for the British to honour the promises made in the McMahon Correspondence.

AN AGREEMENT WITH FRANCE

A month before the start of the Arab revolt in 1916 a secret agreement was made between France and Britain concerning the eventual partition of the Turkish Empire. The discussion which resulted in this agreement took place between Sir Mark Sykes, a British diplomat, and Charles Georges-Picot, formerly French consul in Syria. It is known as the *Sykes-Picot Agreement* and its terms were:

Source 8

1. That France and Great Britain are prepared to recognise and protect an independent Arab state or a Confederation of Arab states in the areas (A) and (B) marked on the annexed map, under the suzerainty of an Arab Chief.

   That in area (A) France and in area (B) Great Britain shall have priority of right of enterprise and local loans.

   That in area (A) France and in area (E) Great Britain shall alone supply advisers or foreign functionaries at the request of the Arab state or Confederation of Arab states.

2. That in the . . . area [marked E on the map] and in the . . . area [marked E on the map] Great Britain shall be allowed to establish such direct or indirect administration or control as they desire and as they may think fit to arrange with the Arab state or Confederation of States.

3. That in the . . . area [marked C on the map] there shall be established an international administration, the form of which is to be decided after consultation with the other allies, and the representatives of the Sherif of Mecca.

4. That Great Britain be accorded (1) the ports of Haifa and Acre [marked E on the map] . . .

   (from W. Laqueur, *The Israel-Arab Reader*)

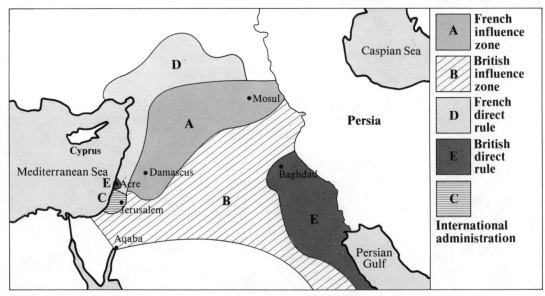

Map 8: The territorial arrangements made by the Sykes-Picot agreement

THE ZIONIST MOVEMENT AND THE BALFOUR DECLARATION

For various reasons, which you may already have discussed after reading the previous sources, Britain was supporting the Arabs in the First World War. However, at the same time the Zionist Movement was gaining support in Britain. Leaders of the Movement, like Chaim Weizmann, claimed Palestine as the historical and spiritual homeland of the Jewish people. They succeeded in influencing some cabinet ministers.

Moreover, in 1917 the British government was anxious to gain the goodwill of the Jewish communities in America and Russia. They hoped that the Jews in America would encourage the United States Government to enter the war on the British and French side, and that Russian Jews would work to keep Russia in the war as an ally of Britain and France. Also, many British officials believed that it was important for Britain to have a community of people living near the Suez Canal who would owe a debt of gratitude to the British.

On 2 November, 1917, the British Foreign Secretary, A. J. Balfour, wrote a letter to Lord Rothschild, an influential member of the Jewish community:

Source 9

Dear Lord Rothschild,

I have much pleasure in conveying to you, on behalf of His Majesty's Government, the following declaration of sympathy with Jewish Zionist aspirations which has been submitted to, and approved by, the Cabinet.

'His Majesty's Government view with favour the establishment in Palestine of a national home for the Jewish people, and will use their best endeavours to facilitate the achievement of this object, it being clearly understood that nothing shall be done which may prejudice the civil and religious rights of existing non-Jewish communities in Palestine, or the rights and political status enjoyed by Jews in any other country.'

I should be grateful if you would bring this declaration to the knowledge of the Zionist Federation.

Yours sincerely,
Arthur James Balfour

Now compare what is said in this letter with the promises made to the Arabs, and the agreement with France. Look at the agreements from the point of view of each of the countries concerned, and from Britain's point of view. Do you think that what Britain had promised was always clearly understood? Would Britain be able to keep her promises to all three? Do you think British policy had changed at all during the war years?

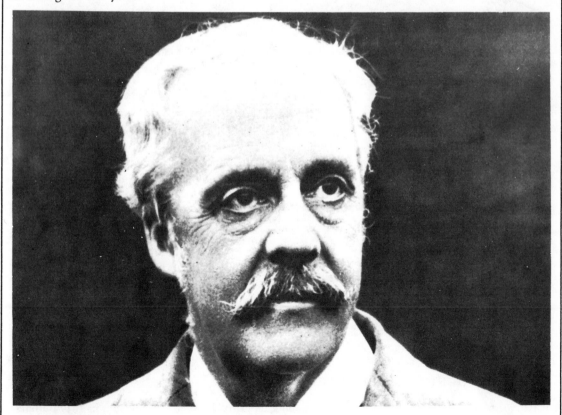

Arthur James Balfour

3 BRITISH RULE IN PALESTINE 1923-1948

THE SITUATION AT THE END OF THE FIRST WORLD WAR

At the Peace Conferences at the end of the war Turkey lost all her Arab lands in the Middle East. The Turkish Empire was divided up and parts of it were entrusted to Britain and France as mandated territories. The mandate system placed the administration of an area under a selected nation until its people were ready to govern themselves. In the Middle East, Britain was to administer Palestine, Iraq and Transjordan while France received Syria and Lebanon.

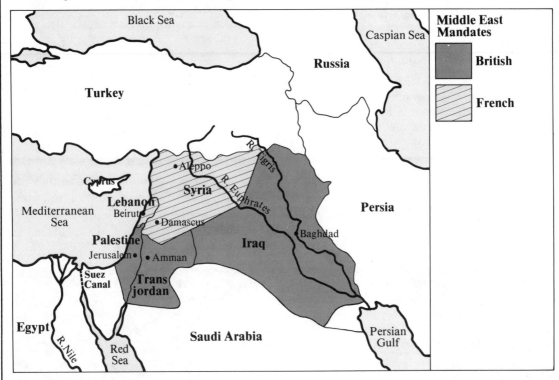

Map 9: Mandated territories in the Middle East in 1923

The San Remo Conference on 24 April, 1920, formally entrusted the government of Palestine to Britain. This arrangement was confirmed by the Council of the League of Nations on 24 July, 1922:

Source 10

The Mandatory [Great Britain] shall be responsible for placing the country under such political, administrative and economic conditions as will secure the establishment of the Jewish national home and the development of self-governing institutions, and also for safeguarding the civil and religious rights of all the inhabitants of Palestine, irrespective of race and religion.

(from W. Laqueur, *The Israel-Arab Reader*)

You can see from this the distinct responsibilities assigned to Britain from September 1923.

PROBLEMS DURING THE BRITISH RULE

Palestine was to prove very difficult to govern and a report of a Royal Commission in 1937 outlined some of the reasons for the unrest between Arabs and Jews:

Source 11

An irrepressible conflict has arisen between two national communities within the narrow bounds of one small country (Palestine). About 1 000 000 Arabs are in strife, open or latent, with some 400 000 Jews. There is no common ground between them. The Arab community is predominantly Asiatic in character, the Jewish community predominantly European. They differ in religion and in language. Their cultural and social life, their ways of thought and conduct, are as incompatible as their national aspirations. These last are the greatest bar to peace. The war of 1914–18 and its sequel have inspired all Arabs with the hope of reviving in a free and united Arab world the traditions of the Arab golden age. The Jews similarly are inspired by their historic past. They mean to show what the Jewish nation can achieve when restored to the land of its birth. National assimilation between Arabs and Jews is thus ruled out. In the Arab picture the Jews could only occupy the place they occupied in Arab Egypt or Arab Spain [in the early middle ages]. The Arabs would be as much outside the Jewish picture as the Canaanites in the old land of Israel. The National Home as we have said before, cannot be half national.

(from W. Laqueur, *The Israel-Arab Reader*)

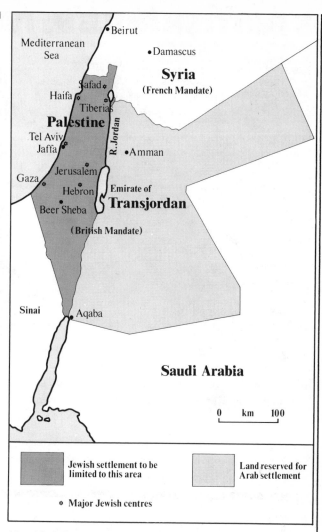

Map 10: Palestine during the British Mandate, 1923–1948

The British defended themselves against Arab accusations by referring to the limitations of Sir Henry McMahon's pledge (look back to his letter p. 15–16).

Jewish immigration

One of the reasons for the bitterness between Jews and Arabs in Palestine throughout the period of the British Mandate was the crucial issue of Jewish immigration. From 1923 to 1939 the British Government supported Jewish settlement in Palestine, as agreed by the terms of the League of Nations mandate:

Source 12

ARTICLE 7 OF THE LEAGUE OF NATIONS MANDATE: 1922

The Administration of Palestine, while ensuring that the rights and position of other sections of the population are not prejudiced, shall facilitate Jewish immigration under suitable conditions and shall encourage, in cooperation with the Jewish Agency, close settlement by the Jews on the land, including State lands and waste lands not required for public purposes.

(from W. Laqueur, *The Israel-Arab Reader*)

Jewish settlers draining swamp land in Palestine in the 1920s

The Arabs, however, became increasingly alarmed at the growth of Jewish immigration, particularly in the years after 1933 when Hitler's policy towards the Jews caused vast numbers to flee from Germany. By 1939 the number of Jews in Palestine had grown to seven times the 1918 figure. The Arabs felt that soon they would be outnumbered by the newcomers and their lands and livelihoods put at risk.

From 1929 onwards there were riots and massacres culminating in a widespread Arab rebellion against British rule between 1936 and 1939. The violence and bitterness between Jew and Arab is expressed in the following story:

Source 13

'AN EYE FOR AN EYE'

In 1945 I visited the Middle East again. I can remember one incident vividly. A swarthy man in a brown suit was sitting next to me at the bar of the Continental Hotel in Cairo, and he offered me a drink.

'You don't mind my addressing you?'

'Heavens no,' I said.

'My friend will be late. And I must wait for half an hour.'

He was about twenty-five years old with heavy, broad shoulders and a wide mouth which seemed set in a perpetual smile.

'I am a Palestinian Jew, you should know,' he said later. 'Does that disturb you?'

'Not at all.'

'But you are English, and the English hate us.'

'Nonsense,' I said. 'Have another drink.'

. . . 'I will tell you something else,' he said in a low voice. 'We Jews hate the English.'

I moved discreetly from his reach.

'We hate them,' he said. As I looked at his eyes I realised what I suppose I should have noticed long before. He was drunk.

'But we hate the Arabs more. Come closer and I will tell you something. But you must promise not to tell anyone.'

'I don't even know your name.'

'You could find out. You could ask people here who know me, couldn't you? Never mind. I don't care. What proof have you got? I will tell you. My father has a factory between Tel-Aviv and Tulkarm, we employ only Jews. Before the war the Arabs used to raid us. There was a hill overlooking the factory. They would lie on this hill and fire at our men. One evening, they killed one of our men. They killed a Jew.'

He drained his glass, and turned round on the bar stool so that he faced me.

'That night in the darkness I went up with one of our foremen who handled the explosives we used for blasting at our works, and together we mined every yard of that hill. We worked until just before dawn when we covered up all trace of our work. But we had concealed a wire from the hillside to the shed which was my office. Each evening I sat in my office by the switch, waiting, waiting for the Arabs to come back.'

His hands were stuck deep into the pockets of his trousers, and he was breathing heavily.

'Each evening I waited. Then one night the Arabs came back. They began firing at our men. But still I waited. I waited until from the flashes I could see there were many of them on the hill. Then I pressed the switch. There was a great flash and a loud explosion. The whole hillside crumbled into the valley. I walked out. The explosion was successful. No Arab body was left whole. I would find the arm of a man here and a leg there. I collected all the remains I could find.'

He paused. His eyes were glittering. Then he finished his story in a voice hoarse with triumph.

'An eye for an eye, and a tooth for a tooth,' he said.
(from R. Maugham, *Approach to Palestine*, Falcon Press, 1947)

British troops dealing with a riot in Palestine, 1937

A CHANGE IN BRITISH POLICY

British policy changed in 1939. Firstly, the British government held a conference in London to discuss the future of Palestine in February 1939. Representatives of the Palestinian Arabs, the Zionists and some Arab states were invited. Like all earlier conferences it was a fiasco. The Palestinian Arabs refused to sit in the same room as the Zionists. As a result parallel sessions had to be held in separate rooms. When the conference collapsed the Government announced that it felt free, in the absence of Arab-Jewish agreement, to enforce its own policy. The British were anxious to pacify the Arabs. They feared the growth of friendship between Germany and some of the Arab leaders. They were anxious to ensure the continuation of oil supplies from Arab countries. If a war was to break out it was essential that the people near the Suez Canal should be friendly and well disposed towards Britain. Accordingly, on 17 May, 1939, the British Government announced its new policy in a White Paper. The following extract from the White Paper shows you Britain's dilemma.

Source 14

The alternatives before His Majesty's Government are either (i) to seek to expand the Jewish National Home indefinitely by immigration, against the strongly expressed will of the Arab people of the country; or (ii) to permit further expansion of the Jewish National Home by immigration only if the Arabs are prepared to acquiesce in it. The former policy means rule by force. Apart from other considerations, such a policy seems to His Majesty's Government to be contrary . . . to their specific obligations to the Arabs in the Palestine Mandate.

(from W. Laqueur, *The Israel-Arab Reader*)

Angry crowds in Jerusalem demonstrate against the White Paper in May 1939

Limitation of Jewish immigration

Jewish immigration was to be limited to 77 000 spread over five years. After that it was to cease altogether unless the Arabs would agree to more. The Jewish reaction was bitterly hostile.

During the war the persecution of Jewish communities in those countries of Europe either under Nazi rule or with governments sympathetic to the Nazis produced a large group of homeless people who wished to enter Palestine. An example of the terror which caused vast numbers of Jews to leave Europe occurred in Rumania in 1941. The pro-Nazi government faced severe opposition from many groups including soldiers of the Fascist Iron Guard. In order to counter this threat the Rumanian Government encouraged attacks on the Jews.

A POGROM IN RUMANIA, 1941

The Nazis scored a complete success. They succeeded in persuading the rebels to organise the pogroms, which cost the Jews over 700 lives. Another 7000 Jews were injured, 2000 of them seriously.

Dozens of Rumanian Jews—women and children as well as men—were literally burned alive by Iron Guard rebels during the Bucharest pogroms last week. Over 200 were foully massacred in a slaughter-house. So declares an eye witness account . . . which states that, apart from those burned to death in hundreds of buildings to which rebel Guards set fire, Jews were beaten senseless in the streets, robbed, then douched with petrol and set on fire.

Perhaps the most horrifying single episode of the pogrom, says the report, was the kosher butchery of more than 200 Jews in a municipal slaughter-house. The Jews, who had been rounded up after several hours of Iron Guard raids, were put into trucks and carried off to the slaughter-house. There Green Shirts forced them to undress and led them to chopping blocks, where they cut their throats in a horrible parody of Shechita [Jewish ritual slaughter of animals]. Tiring of this sport after a few score had been slaughtered, forty to fifty armed soldiers, mad with hate, beheaded the rest with axes and knives.

(*Jewish Chronicle*, 31 January 1941)

German SS men cutting the hair of Russian Jew before beating him to death

Jewish refugees from Europe in 1946. They hoped to land in Palestine in spite of immigration restrictions

Illegal immigration to Palestine

The illegal immigration of Jews into Palestine increased after World War Two (1939–45). The British forces in Palestine intercepted many Jews who were seeking illegal entry. For example in 1947 the ship *Exodus* was rammed by a British destroyer as it tried to break the blockade and land 4500 Jewish refugees from German camps. The British Government ordered all the refugees on the *Exodus* to be returned to Displaced Persons Camps in Germany.

At the trials of war criminals at Nuremburg after the war many people gave evidence of the horrors of Nazi concentration camps. This is the testimony of the Commandant of Auschwitz extermination camp:

Source 16

The 'Final solution' of the Jewish question meant the complete extermination of all Jews in Europe. I was ordered to establish extermination facilities at Auschwitz in June 1941.

. . . I visited Treblinka to find out how they carried out their extermination. The Camp Commandant told me that he had liquidated eighty thousand in the course of one half year. He was principally concerned with liquidating all the Jews from the Warsaw ghetto. He used monoxide gas and I did not think that his methods were very efficient. So at Auschwitz I used Cyclon B, which was a crystallized prussic acid dropped into the death chamber. It took from three to fifteen minutes to kill the people in the chamber, according to climatic conditions. We knew when the people were dead because their screaming stopped. We usually waited about half an hour before we opened the doors and removed the bodies. After the bodies were removed our special commandos took off the rings and extracted the gold from the teeth of the corpses. Another improvement that we made over Treblinka was that we built our gas chambers to accommodate two thousand people at one time . . .

(*Nuremburg Documents*)

Inmates of a German concentration camp

Guerrilla war in Palestine

Such revelations helped to generate widespread sympathy for the demand that Jewish survivors from Nazi Europe should be freely admitted to Palestine. A campaign of violence was waged by Jewish terrorist groups—the Irgun and Stern Gang—to force the British Government to remove immigration restrictions. A full scale guerrilla war developed between the British army and Zionist forces, as well as periodic violence between Arab and Jew. The British Government made a final attempt to secure Arab-Jewish agreement by direct talks. This time both the Zionists and the Palestine Arabs refused to attend. The Foreign Secretary, Ernest Bevin, explained Britain's attitude in a speech to the House of Commons on the 18th of February, 1947:

Source 17

For the Arabs the fundamental point is that Palestine should no longer be denied the independence which has now been attained by every other Arab State; they regard the further expansion of the Jewish National Home as jeopardising the attainment and they are therefore unwilling to contemplate further Jewish immigration into Palestine. They are equally opposed to the creation of a Jewish state in any part of Palestine.

The Jewish Agency, on the other hand, have made it clear that their fundamental aim is the creation of an independent Jewish State in Palestine. With this in view they first proposed that His Majesty's Government should continue to adminis-ter the mandate on a basis which would enable them to continue to expand the Jewish National Home until such time as they had attained by immigration a numerical majority in Palestine and could demand the creation of an independent Jewish State over the country as a whole.

His Majesty's Government have of themselves no power, under the terms of the Mandate, to award the country either to the Arabs or to the Jews, or even to partition it between them. We have, therefore, reached the conclusion that the only course now open to us is to submit the problem to the judgement of the United Nations.

(from R. Maugham, *Approach to Palestine*)

King David Hotel, Jerusalem, July 1946. This building, used as a British Military Headquarters, was dynamited by Jewish terrorists

Partition of Palestine and the State of Israel

In November 1947, the United Nations General Assembly voted for the partition of Palestine into Arab and Jewish States. The Zionists accepted this proposal, but the Arabs rejected it. The UN could not enforce it. In the event it was enforced by the Israeli Army. On 14 May, 1948, the State of Israel was proclaimed.

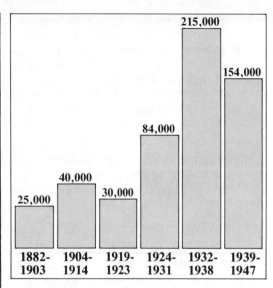

i. Jewish immigration into Palestine
1882–1947

Date	No. of Jews	Total Population	Percentage of Jews
1918	60,000	700,000	9%
1931	175,000	1,036,000	18%
1939	429,605	1,500,000	28%
1947	650,000	2,000,000	32%

ii. Jews in Palestine in proportion to the
total population

Crowds in Tel Aviv celebrating the UN vote on the State of Israel

4 THE INTERNAL DEVELOPMENT OF ISRAEL FROM 1948

THE PROCLAMATION OF THE STATE OF ISRAEL

The Independence of the State of Israel was proclaimed in Tel Aviv on 14 May, 1948. The proclamation justifies the existence of the new state in the following terms:

Source 18

The land of Israel was the birthplace of the Jewish people. Here their spiritual, religious and national identity was formed. Here they achieved independence and created a culture of national and universal significance. Here they wrote and gave the Bible to the world.

Exiled from the Land of Israel the Jewish people remained faithful to it in all the countries of their dispersion, never ceasing to pray and hope for their return and the restoration of their national freedom.

Impelled by this historic association, Jews strove throughout the centuries to go back to the land of their fathers and regain their statehood. In recent decades they returned in their masses. They reclaimed the wilderness, revived their language, built cities and villages, and established a vigorous and ever-growing community, with its own economic and cultural life. They sought peace, yet were prepared to defend themselves. They brought the blessings of progress to all inhabitants of the country and looked forward to sovereign independence.

... On 29 November 1947, the General Assembly of the United Nations adopted a Resolution requiring the establishment of a Jewish State in Palestine. The General Assembly called upon the inhabitants of the country to take all the necessary steps on their part to put the plan into effect. This recognition by the United Nations of the right of the Jewish people to establish their independent State is unassailable.

It is the natural right of the Jewish people to lead, as do all other nations, an independent existence in its sovereign State.

(from W. Laqueur, *The Israel-Arab Reader*)

David Ben-Gurion proclaiming the State of Israel, May 1948

However, some Jews give different reasons for their right to the land. In a television programme, prepared in 1975 by an Egyptian journalist and an Israeli T.V. producer, an Israeli writer, A. B. Yehoshua, gave his reasons for defending his country:

Source 19

I don't believe in the Jews' historical right to come back and take land from other people because we were here 2000 years ago. Instead, we have the right because of the Holocaust. We have a right to part of this country and the Palestinians have a right to theirs.

In 1949 the Israeli Parliament (Knesset) moved from Tel Aviv to Jerusalem where its new building had been completed. Jerusalem was proclaimed capital of Israel in the same year. David Ben Gurion was the first Prime Minister.

The Knesset: the Jewish parliament building in Jerusalem

THE 'LAW OF RETURN'

One of the main concerns of the new State has been to attract Jewish immigrants to Israel. The 'Law of Return', which was passed unanimously by the Knesset in July 1950, states:

Source 20

1. Every Jew has the right to immigrate to the country.

2. (a) Immigration shall be on the basis of immigration visas.

   (b) Immigrant visas shall be issued to any Jew expressing a desire to settle in Israel, except if the Ministry of Immigration is satisfied that the applicant:

   (i) acts against the Jewish nation; or

   (ii) may threaten the public health or State security.

3. (a) A Jew who comes to Israel and after his arrival expresses a desire to settle there may, while in

Israel, obtain an immigrant certificate.

(b) The exceptions listed in Article 2(b) shall apply also with respect to the issue of an immigrant certificate, but a person shall not be regarded as a threat to public health as a result of an illness that he contracts after his arrival in Israel.

4. Every Jew who migrated to the country before this law goes into effect, and every Jew who was born in the country either before or after the law is effective enjoys the same status as any person who migrated on the basis of this law.

(from W. Laqueur, *The Israel-Arab Reader*)

INCREASING POPULATION IN ISRAEL

The population in Israel has increased four times since 1948. This has been due partly to natural population increase and partly to immigration policies. There was a huge influx of immigrants from Europe between 1948 and 1950.

Many Jewish immigrants also came to Israel from Arab countries in the Middle East. However, the initial high rate of immigration was not sustained and there was a considerable decrease in the number of newcomers after 1955. In 1969 Israel's Jewish population numbered over two and a half million. The percentage of Jews in the total population of Israel has varied between 85 per cent and 90 per cent.

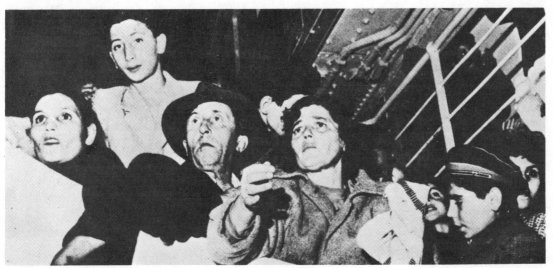

Jews from Europe arrive in their new homeland in 1951

1948	770,000
1954	1,717,814
1961	2,232,300
1969	2,841,100
1973	3,200,000

i. The growth of the population of Israel 1948–1973

1949	239,000
1955	110,000
1959	60,000
1965	50,000
1968	40,000

ii. Jewish immigration into Israel 1949–1968

THE INFLUENCE OF THE JEWISH RELIGION

The influence of the Jewish religion is strong in Israel, just as it was in Jewish communities during the Dispersion. There are two chief religious leaders of the Jewish people in Israel. One of these Rabbis has jurisdiction over the Jews who originally came from Europe. Another looks after those Jews who came from North Africa and the Middle East. These religious leaders have considerable responsibilities and power. Their courts have jurisdiction over marriage and divorce, the observance of the Sabbath (Saturday), the protection of the holy places, the synagogues (churches) and the observance of laws about food.

Many religious leaders play a prominent part in politics in Israel. Since 1948 most governments have only been able to maintain power by including some of these religious leaders in the cabinet and practising policies acceptable to them. The Government, through a Minister of religious affairs, is responsible for providing religious facilities for all creeds. One section of the Ministry supervises all Jewish religious affairs while the other cares for the needs of non-Jewish minorities, like the Muslims and Christians.

Rabbis reading the Jewish Law in a synogogue

MILITARY DEFENCE

Another of the main concerns of Israel has been military defence. The aim has been to create an army which has the most modern equipment and is in a constant state of readiness. In 1950, 44 per cent of the whole of government expenditure was on defence. In the financial year 1974–5 once again 44 per cent was earmarked for defence purposes. Both men and women have to undertake National Service. Men serve for 30 months, though women serve for less. After military service a man becomes a soldier again in the reserve for up to two months in every year, until he is 45 years old.

ECONOMIC DEVELOPMENT

There has been a remarkable expansion of the Israeli economy since 1948. This has been partly due to the increase in population which has provided a large work force. There has also been a rapid development of industry particularly in oil, chemicals, wines, shipbuilding and automobile manufacture. Many scientific research projects have contributed to the industrial progress.

Although Israel has experienced some difficulty in finding foreign markets—particularly in Arab countries and some Communist states—her exports have increased enormously. The bulk of Israel's export earnings has come from sales of citrus fruits and polished diamonds. Other products playing an increasingly important role in export sales include textiles, processed foods, chemical products, electronic equipment, fertilisers and plastic goods. Israel's main customers are the USA and Britain. The tourist industry is developing although the periodic wars since 1948 have disrupted its progress.

AGRICULTURE AND THE KIBBUTZIM

There has also been rapid agricultural improvement. Since 1948 about 500 new agricultural settlements have been established. Particularly noteworthy has been the development of areas which were extremely unfavourable to agriculture. As David Ben Gurion once said, 'If Israel doesn't put an end to the desert, the desert will put an end to Israel'. In the Negev desert there have been large scale reclamation schemes. Care has been taken to put the meagre water supplies to full use. Tree plantation schemes have helped to prevent soil erosion.

By 1969 the area of land under cultivation in Israel was four times what it was when independence was declared.

Two particular types of agricultural villages have developed in Israel. In the *Kibbutzim* (collective farms) everything is shared. These settlements often have over one hundred families living there. All members of working age work for the community without wages. The entire income from the farm, together with any other communal enterprise, goes into a common fund controlled by the members. Members live in houses built, owned and maintained by the Kibbutz which also provides their clothes, food and health and education services. Meals are taken in a communal dining room. By 1972 there were about 230 Kibbutzim in Israel with about 2 per cent of the population living in them.

The Negev Desert

Workers in a tree nursery in the Negev, from which shrubs are transplanted into the desert

35

The other type of farm settlement is the *Moshav* village. The cooperation between the members is similar to the Kibbutz but in these villages each family owns its own house and land.

Kibbutz Sheluhot in the Beit Shean region of Israel

5 THE DEVELOPMENT OF EGYPT

After World War Two a strong nationalist movement developed in Egypt. By the terms of the Anglo-Egyptian treaty of 1936 the British were permitted to keep a garrison of 10 000 soldiers in the Suez Canal zone for 20 years. Many Egyptians resented this and other signs of British influence.

Moreover, there was widespread dissatisfaction with the ruler of Egypt, King Farouk. Many believed that the King was concerned only with his own selfish extravagant pleasures. The King's ministers were composed of rich men who cared little for the extreme poverty of most of the Egyptian people. The King and government were further discredited by the defeat of Egyptian forces in the 1948–9 war.

BIOGRAPHY: KING FAROUK

King Farouk ruled Egypt from 1936 to 1952. He was educated in Egypt and England before he became King. After the outbreak of World War II (1939–45) he tried to keep Egypt neutral although there were British troops in Egypt.

In 1948, the newly created state of Israel defeated Egypt and injured the pride of the growing number of Egyptian nationalists. Many army officers considered that King Farouk's misgovernment was the real cause of Egypt's weakness. A group called the Free Officers, overthrew King Farouk in July 1952 and he went into exile. He died in Rome in 1965.

A British Camp on the Canal Zone, 1951

President Nasser with Mr Krushchev of Russia, 1964

EGYPT UNDER PRESIDENT NASSER

In July 1952 the Egyptian revolution took place. A group of army officers led by General Neguib forced King Farouk to abdicate and took over the government of the country. The Republic of Egypt was proclaimed.

In 1954 Gamal Abdul Nasser succeeded Neguib as Prime Minister. In 1956 he became President of Egypt. Nasser promised great social changes. He set about destroying the power of the large landowners and redistributing the land more fairly. He was determined to remove the influence of Britain in Egypt, and he was successful in negotiating the withdrawal of British troops from the Canal Zone.

The Canal Zone

Nasser was determined to build a high dam across the Nile at Aswan. As only 3·5 per cent of the total land area of Egypt was cultivable at this time, water from the dam would greatly increase agricultural productivity. It could also be used to generate hydro-electric power.

In 1953 Egypt opened negotiations with the World Bank to secure a loan to enable construction of the dam to continue. American influence at the World Bank was strong and they feared that Egypt was rapidly coming under Russian influence. This was confirmed in 1955 when Nasser made an agreement with Communist Czechoslovakia for the purchase of arms. In 1956 the World Bank refused to make a loan.

Oil tanker passing through the Suez Canal

Nationalisation of the Suez Canal

Nasser then sought alternative sources of revenue and support. In July 1956 he seized control of the Suez Canal. The Canal had previously been run by a company whose shareholders came mainly from Britain and France and included the British Government. The income from tolls from traffic through the Canal was to be used to build the Aswan High Dam. On 26 July, 1956, President Nasser formally announced the nationalisation of the Suez Canal Company:

Source 21

The Suez Canal Company sitting in Paris, is a usurping company. It usurped our concessions . . . We shall build the High Dam and we shall gain our usurped rights. We shall build the High Dam as we desire. We are determined. The Canal Company annually takes £35 000 000. Why shouldn't we take it ourselves? . . .

As I told you a little while ago, it is no shame to be poor and to strive and build my country. What is shameful, however, is to suck blood. They sucked our blood, and extorted and stole our rights. Today, as we retrieve these rights, I declare on behalf of the Egyptian people that we shall preserve these rights and cherish them . . . We shall protect these rights because thereby we shall be making up for the past. As we build the edifice of grandeur, freedom and dignity we feel that it can never be built or become complete unless we demolish the facades

of oppression, humiliation and degradation. The Suez Canal was one of the facades of oppression, extortion and humiliation. Today, O citizens, the Suez Canal has been nationalised . . .Today, O citizens, we declare that our property has been returned to us. The rights about which we were silent have been restored to us. Today, citizens, with the annual income of the Suez Canal amounting to £35 000 000 . . . We shall not look for . . . American aid . . . Your Egyptian brethren . . . have started to take over the Canal Company and its property and to control shipping through the canal—the canal which is owned by Egypt.

(from *Documents of International Affairs 1956* edited by Noble Frankland and published by Oxford University Press, 1959)

The nationalisation of the Suez Canal was one of the main factors in the development of the crisis which resulted in the war of October and November 1956 (see below, page 43). Nasser had staked his political career on building the Aswan dam. The revenues from the Canal, after it had been cleared of blockships by March 1957, and technical assistance and loans from Russia helped to complete the construction of the dam. At the dedication ceremony in 1971 the guest of honour was President Podgorny of Russia.

The Aswan High Dam

Economic development

Although the building of the dam was Nasser's most spectacular achievement his domestic policies resulted in other successes. Much of the land had been transferred to the people. No one was allowed to have more than 100 acres [40·5 hectares] of land. Land reclamation and irrigation schemes had increased agricultural production. The school building and welfare programmes in the countryside had had much success. Industries—particularly oil and cotton production—had been developed and factories and banks under foreign influence had been nationalised.

Nasser was the first native-born ruler of Egypt since the Pharaohs, apart from General Neguib. He could justly claim that he had achieved the changes for which he had worked—'a political revolution against imperialism and a social revolution against feudalism, monopoly and exploitation'. Nevertheless, his successor, President Anwar Sadat, inherited grave domestic problems in 1970. For example, the huge annual population increase and the heavy expenditure on defence posed serious difficulties. There was also considerable criticism of the way Nasser had restricted the individual freedom of the Egyptian people.

Leadership of the Arab world

During his period of rule 1954–1970 President Nasser made a bid for the leadership of the Arab world. He achieved much success in this role. Many Arabs in other countries of the Middle East, like Syria and Iraq wished to copy his domestic reforms in Egypt in their own states. Nasser made full use of radio and the press. His broadcasts and newspapers from Cairo ensured that his personality and views were known all over the Arab world—from Algeria in the west to the Persian Gulf in the east. Moreover, the way Egypt met the challenge from Britain, France and Israel in the Suez Crisis of 1956 won him immense popularity (see below, page 43). He became a focus for Arab Nationalism.

Nasser developed the idea of a League of Arab States. This had first formed in Cairo in 1945 with members from Egypt, Iraq, Transjordan, Yemen, Saudi Arabia, Syria and Lebanon. Nasser was determined to establish a permanent Arab League which would shape common Arab policies. In 1958 he set up the United Arab Republic which included Egypt and Syria. This initial scheme was a failure and Syria left the union in 1961. However, the idea was revived in April 1963 and an attempt was made to establish a federated Arab State consisting of Egypt, Iraq and Syria. This scheme also failed.

At the invitation of President Nasser representatives of the thirteen Arab League countries met in Cairo in January 1964. Regular conferences were held in subsequent years. There was much ill feeling in these meetings. But hostility to Israel, a boycott of all Israeli goods, and support for the Palestine refugees provided areas of agreement.

President Nasser came near to his goal of uniting the Arab world. But in the last three years of his life hostility from his fellow Arabs grew. The Arab failure in the 1967 war with Israel (see below page 46) was a severe blow to his prestige. After the war many Arabs became increasingly hostile to Nasser's apparent readiness to make a settlement with Israel. Nasser's interference in the internal affairs of other Arab states—like Saudi Arabia, Tunisia and Jordan—brought increasing criticism. Egypt's reliance on Russian military and economic aid displeased many Arabs in the Middle East. The various Arab States not only had widely differing aims and policies at home and abroad, but their leaders were often jealous of Nasser. There were also violent revolutions in most of the Arab States in the Middle East during this period. These prevented the development of common Arab policies. However, in October 1973 during the fourth Arab-Israeli war, the Arab states succeeded in establishing a common policy concerning the sale of oil to the Western World.

Anwar Sadat, Nasser's successor as President of Egypt

40

6 FOUR WARS IN TWENTY-FIVE YEARS

The story of the Arab countries and Israel from 1948 is one of continuous hostility. The Arab-Israeli dispute has erupted into war four times in one generation—in 1948-9, 1956, 1967 and 1973. A brief survey of these wars and the crises from which they developed not only helps us to understand an important aspect of the conflict; it provides a framework in which to view the whole story of the relations between Arabs and Jews in the Middle East since 1948.

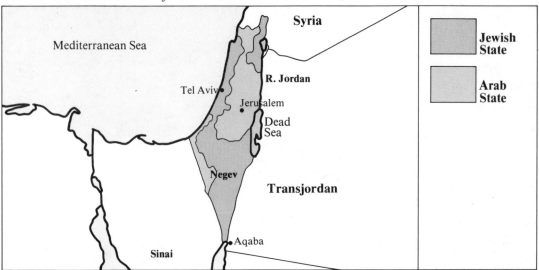

Map 11: The UN partition plan for Palestine

THE FIRST WAR, 1948-9

It is difficult to say exactly when the first Arab-Jewish war began. When the British government announced in February 1947 that it was handing over the Mandate of Palestine to the United Nations, skirmishes between Arab and Jewish guerrillas became fiercer. In November 1947 the United Nations decided that Palestine would be partitioned into Arab and Jewish states. The violence continued as the British troops began to withdraw from Palestine. For example, in April 1948 Jewish terrorists destroyed the Arab village of Deir Yassin, near Jerusalem, and massacred the inhabitants.

An Egyptian stamp commenting on the Israeli terrorist attack on the Arab village of Deir Yassin, April 1948

The new State of Israel was proclaimed 14 May, 1948. Immediately the armies of the Arab countries of Egypt, Lebanon, Iraq, Syria and Transjordan invaded Israel. Their aim was to seize control of the whole of the area of Palestine and destroy Israel. A state of war now formally existed.

41

Three phases of the war

The war fell into three phases. The first lasted for 37 days until the United Nations mediator, Count Bernadotte, called a truce on 11 June. During the first phase the Israeli armies were able to hold a five-fold Arab attack but lost the Jewish quarter of Jerusalem.

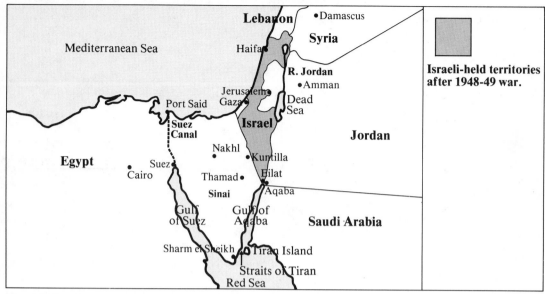

Map 12: The Arab States and Israel, 1949–1967

A ten-day war in July formed the second phase. Israeli forces gained control in the north to the Lebanese border and also re-occupied the western sector of Jerusalem. On 18 July a second truce was imposed.

The third phase of the war began in October. In late December the final campaign of the war in Israeli territory was fought.

An Israeli victory

Israel's forces had foiled the attempt to drive them out of Palestine and had expelled the Arab armies from Israeli soil. They had also occupied some of the land which had been allocated to the Arabs by the UN partition plan of 1947. Armistices were signed between the Arab states and Israel by the summer of 1949, but no peace settlement was made. Israel refused to hand back the lands she occupied. The Arab states refused to recognise the State of Israel and asserted that they were still in a state of war with her.

There were many reasons for the Israeli victory. The Jewish people, whether settlers of long standing or recent immigrants from post-war Europe, had a fanatical determination to survive. Their ancestors had lacked a home for nearly 2000 years, and they were fighting to establish Israel as their homeland. Their morale was high because of the immediate recognition of Israel by President Truman of America in May 1948 and the enormous financial help and other gifts from Jewish people in Europe and America.

The Israeli army was well organised, tenacious and dedicated. The members of the Jewish terrorist groups were experienced and hardened by their operations against the British forces and Arabs during the period of the Mandate. Although the Jewish army was smaller in numbers than the Arab forces it was slightly better armed. Some of the military equipment—field guns, small tanks, automatic rifles and machine guns—was purchased from Czechoslovakia. The Israeli army was well led. Lieutenant-Colonel Moshe Dayan was one of the commanders.

The Arab invasion was hampered by military inexperience and by rivalry between the armies of each state. Their lines of communication were over-extended and military and medical supplies were uncertain. Most of the Arab military leaders were not effective although a young Egyptian officer, Major Nasser, distinguished himself by his skill and bravery.

THE WAR OF 1956

Relations between Israel and the Arab states remained hostile after 1949. One of the main sources of friction was the repeated raids of Egyptian terrorists (or *fedayeen* which means 'self-sacrificers') into Israeli territory. In February 1955, Israel's new Defence Minister, Ben Gurion, ordered a massive retaliatory raid against Egyptian military installations in Gaza. The Egyptians refused to allow Israeli ships to pass through the Suez Canal. From the strong point of Sharm-el-Sheikh, the Egyptians prevented Israeli ships from entering the straits of Tiran. The Arab countries boycotted Israeli goods and would not permit Israeli planes to cross Arab territory.

The Suez Crisis

The Egyptian leader, President Nasser, aimed to re-equip the Egyptian army and to negotiate with the World Bank for a loan to construct the Aswan High Dam on the River Nile. In September 1955 he made an agreement with Communist Czechoslovakia for the purchase of military equipment. It soon became clear that these arms had actually come from Russia. This alarmed the Americans who hoped to limit Communist influence in the Middle East. In July 1956, Mr Dulles, the US Secretary of State, responded by withdrawing American support at the World Bank for the loan for Egypt's dam project. President Nasser retaliated by seizing the Suez Canal and declaring it Egyptian property. The Canal had been run, hitherto, by a company whose administrators and shareholders were mainly British and French. Nasser announced that the profits from the Canal would help to finance the dam.

The British and French governments were bitterly hostile to the nationalisation of the Canal as it endangered their vital oil supplies from the Middle East which passed through the Canal. Sir Anthony Eden, the British Prime Minister, declared that Nasser should not be allowed 'to have his thumb on our windpipe'. Moreover both governments, like their American allies, disliked the growth of Russian influence in Egypt. Sir Anthony Eden regarded Nasser as the would-be Hitler of the Nile and the French government also resented Egyptian assistance to the Algerian nationalists who began their rebellion against France in 1954. Frenzied diplomatic activity took place at the United Nations in New York and between the leaders of Britain, France, Russia and the USA but no progress was made towards peace.

Map 13: The Suez campaign

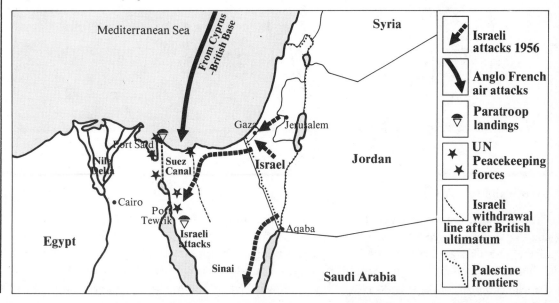

The Israeli invasion of Egypt, October 1956

On 29 October, 1956, Israeli forces invaded Egypt. The battle plan of the Israeli Chief of Staff, Moshe Dayan, was successfully put into operation. The Egyptian border bases at Ras-en-Nakeb, Kuntilla and Kusseima were occupied and Israeli paratroops took up positions in the Mitla Pass. Soon Israeli troops captured Gaza and the Mitla Pass was taken. On 5 November, Sharm-el-Sheikh surrendered. The drive to Sharm-el-Sheikh has become one of the epics of Israeli military history. The Israeli force, which was made up of 200 vehicles and 1000 men had sufficient food and water for only five days. Any major mishap along the 288 kilometre drive could have brought disaster. The army moved onward in spite of the road surface which was melting in the heat and sometimes engulfed by deep sand. At Sharm-el-Sheikh the army, aided by air support, destroyed the Egyptian gun emplacements. The whole of Sinai was now in Israeli hands and the depleted Egyptian forces (for many soldiers had been withdrawn to face the British and French attack in the Canal Zone) had been defeated. Egypt's plan for the defence of Sinai had failed.

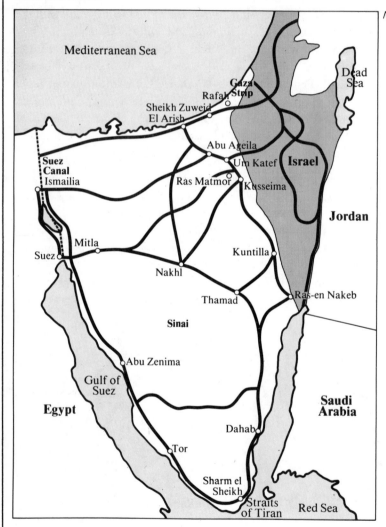

Map 14: The Sinai campaign, 1956

Britain and France intervene

On 30 October, Britain and France issued a 12 hour ultimatum, threatening to intervene if the Egyptians and Israelis did not agree to a ceasefire and withdraw to positions 10 miles (16 kilometres) on each side of the Suez Canal. Egypt did not comply and an Anglo-French attack followed. On 31 October, British and French aircraft began bombing Egyptian airfields. Five days later British and French troops parachuted into Port Said. On 6 November the Anglo-French seaborne troops landed and began to advance down the Canal. Egypt retaliated by sinking ships to block the Canal.

Then the Russians made a decisive move, threatening to intervene in the war with rocket attacks against the Israeli and Anglo-French forces. The United States brought pressure on Britain and France and a ceasefire was declared on 6 November. British and French forces gradually withdrew and were replaced by a United Nations Emergency Force.

Gains and losses

Israel agreed to withdraw her forces from the Gaza Strip and Sharm-el-Sheikh in 1957. But though they made no territorial gains from the war, the Israelis had destroyed the Egyptian arms supremacy. Much of the equipment acquired in the Czech arms deal had been captured or destroyed in the Sinai campaign. The Israelis also gained the knowledge that they could defeat the Arabs on the battlefield.

The Egyptians had suffered a defeat but President Nasser was able to say that the Israelis had succeeded only because of the combined attack of Britain and France. The Suez war convinced the Arabs that Israel was in league with the western powers. There was very little goodwill for Britain left in the Arab world. Meanwhile Russia had greatly increased her influence in the Middle East.

British newspapers, 31 October 1956

45

Israeli troops examine tanks abandoned by the Egyptians during the war of 1956

THE SIX DAY WAR OF 1967

After the Suez War of 1956 both Israel and the Arab countries increased their military strength. The Egyptians and the Syrians received military equipment—including submarines, MiG jets, jet bombers, tanks and missiles—from Russia. Israel purchased Mystère and Mirage aeroplanes from the French and tanks from Britain, as well as a vast range of military supplies from the USA.

The crisis builds up

The crisis which led to the June war of 1967 had been building up for six months. A guerrilla force of Palestinian Arabs, known as Al-Fatah, operating from Jordan and Syria, began to carry out raids into Israel. Israel retaliated by punitive attacks on Al-Fatah bases in Jordan. Meanwhile, Syrian artillery were continually bombarding Israeli farm workers from the Golan Heights. In April 1967 Israel responded by an air attack on the Syrian positions.

President Nasser came under increasing criticism from the other leaders for not taking sterner measures against Israel. Accordingly, on 19 May, 1967, Nasser requested that the United Nations Emergency Force which had been in the Canal Zone since 1956 should be withdrawn. The Secretary-General of the United Nations, U Thant, agreed. At a brief ceremony in Gaza, the blue and white flag of the United Nations was lowered and the soldiers from various countries, including India, Canada, Yugoslavia and Sweden, left the Middle East. Egyptian troops moved up and occupied Sharm-el-Sheikh. On 23 May, President Nasser announced that the Straits of Tiran had been closed to Israeli ships. He stated, 'The Israeli flag will no longer pass the gulf of Aqaba; our sovereignty over the gulf is indisputable. If Israel threatens us with war, we will reply thus "Go ahead, then".' Following the Egyptian announcement there was great diplomatic activity involving Britain, France, the USA and Russia as well as the Middle East countries but although some pressure was brought to bear on President Nasser to reverse his decision, he stayed firm over the Tiran blockade.

Meanwhile, the Egyptian and Syrian governments had declared that their forces were 'in combat readiness' and the troops of Jordan, Iraq and Kuwait had been mobilised. Israel had also completed partial mobilisation. On 26 May, President Nasser announced that if war came Israel would be totally destroyed. Military help for the Arab cause was also promised by Algeria and the Sudan. On 30 May, King Hussein of Jordan flew to Cairo and signed a defence agreement with President Nasser. The Arab press and radio stations continued their bitter attack on Israel. Syrian radio announced to Israel that, 'we have decided to drench this land with . . . blood, to oust you, aggressors, and throw you into the sea for good'.

Israeli army tanks on manoeuvres in the desert, May 1967

The watch tower in this Israeli Kibbutz is manned night and day to give advance warning of mortar attacks from Arab guerrillas over the Jordanian border nearby

Egyptian troops awaiting orders, Sharm el Sheikh May, 1967

The Israelis' attack and victory

The Israeli government, advised by Moshe Dayan who became Defence Minister on 1 June, decided to strike first. On the morning of 5 June, Israel attacked with savage force.

General Dayan (right) enters the conquered city of Bethlehem in Jordan's West Bank area, June 1967

Within six days it was all over. Egypt had been pushed back behind the Suez Canal. Jordan had been forced to evacuate the area west of the Jordan river, and the Syrians were driven from the Golan Heights. There were many factors which contributed to the decisive victory of the Israeli forces. Probably the most important reason for the Israeli success was her total command of the air throughout the six-day campaign. On 5 June, within four hours, the Egyptian air force was destroyed by Israeli air strikes. Nineteen airfields were attacked. The Israeli pilots also crippled the Syrian, Jordanian and Iraqi airforces on the same day.

A detachment of the Israeli army advances past a truck carrying Egyptian prisoners during the June war of 1967

The Sinai campaign

In the Sinai desert the Israeli armoured forces with air support fought a brilliant campaign. They seized and held the initiative throughout. By 7 June Israeli forces were in command of the entire Sinai desert. The Egyptian commanders were not able to match the skill of the Israelis. The heaviest Israeli casualties occurred in the battle with the Jordanian army in the Arab sector in Jerusalem. The Jordanian army retreated across the Jordan river. The Israelis mounted an offensive against Syria and her forces were driven from the Golan Heights.

THE WANDERING ARAB

Thousands of Egyptians, remnants of an army recruited from the deprived and oppressed of centuries, have perished in the Sinai Desert.

A Punch *cartoon of 21 June 1967, commenting on the Arab defeat in the Six Day War*

The Arab forces had been stronger than those of Israel with far more men, tanks and aircraft. However, in the war the Arabs failed to make the best use of their modern equipment. Once again Israeli military planning proved superior.

On 10 June a cease-fire was accepted, but no permanent peace was achieved. The Arab states continued to refuse to recognise Israel and demanded that the territories occupied in the war should be returned. Israel was determined to retain these territories as they provided strong and defensible borders.

BIOGRAPHY: MOSHE DAYAN

Moshe Dayan was born in Palestine in 1915. He joined the *Haganah* (the Jewish underground organisation) at the age of 14 and was jailed by the British for terrorist activities in 1939. He was released after serving only one year of his ten-year sentence, and joined the British army during the Second World War. He went on commando raids against French forces in Syria which had collaborated with the Germans. In an attack he lost his left eye and acquired a black eye patch which became his trade mark.

In the 1948–9 Arab-Israeli war Dayan fought as commander of a jeep commando battalion on the Jerusalem front.

However, it was as Chief of Staff during the Sinai campaign of 1956 that he became a popular hero in Israel and won international fame. He has told his story of the Sinai victory in his book *Diary of the Sinai Campaign, 1956*, which was published in Britain in 1966.

Dayan was responsible for the brilliant success of the Israeli forces during the Six Day War. He appreciated the importance of swift air strikes early in the war to secure command of the skies, and was able to coordinate the work of the army and the air force. He proved an energetic and inspiring leader.

After the Six Day War, Dayan continued to play an important part in Israeli and international politics. He strongly asserted that Israel should retain all the territories she had occupied in 1967. He also worked with Golda Meir, the Prime Minister, to improve Israel's military equipment. Dayan took a firm stand against any compromises with the Arab states. He became the leader of the group of politicians in Israel known as the 'hawks', bitterly opposing the policies of the 'doves' who were prepared to make concessions in negotiations for peace with the Arabs.

During the war of October 1973 Dayan was Defence Minister. After the war began he was criticised by some in Israel for being over-confident and not anticipating the Arab attack despite all the signs of a military invasion. Nevertheless, once hostilities were under way most agreed that he organised the Israeli war effort with his usual flair.

After the 1973 Yom Kippur war, there was widespread criticism of General Dayan because of Israel's allegedly inadequate military preparations. These, it was said, had enabled the Egyptian and Syrian armies to make important gains during the first few days of the war. There was a demand for his resignation.

Despite support for Dayan from Golda Meir, the Cabinet decided to set up a Judicial Commission to investigate the conduct of the war. The Interim Report of the Commission found that General Dayan was not responsible for the delay in mobilising the reserves at the outbreak of the war. Despite this, the Labour Party (the majority party in the government) was split over whether Dayan should resign as Minister of Defence.

The situation was resolved when the new government, formed by General Rabin after the resignation of Mrs Meir as Prime Minister, excluded General Dayan. Probably because of Dayan's continued 'hard line' attitude to the Arabs he has not been reinstated in office by Rabin's Government which is trying to negotiate a compromise peace with Israel's neighbours.

THE WAR OF YOM KIPPUR, 1973

Fighting on land, sea and air broke out along the Egyptian and Syrian 1967 cease-fire lines on 6 October 1973. Egyptian and Syrian forces attacked on the most sacred day in the Jewish religious calendar, Yom Kippur, the Day of Atonement. In many cases the Israelis mobilised their army and reserves from the synagogues.

Arab forces crossed the east bank of the Suez Canal and established bridgeheads. Meanwhile Syrian forces attacked with heavy artillery support along the 96 kilometre length of the Golan Heights which

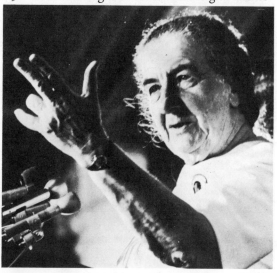

Golda Meir, Prime Minister of Israel at the time of the Yom Kippur War

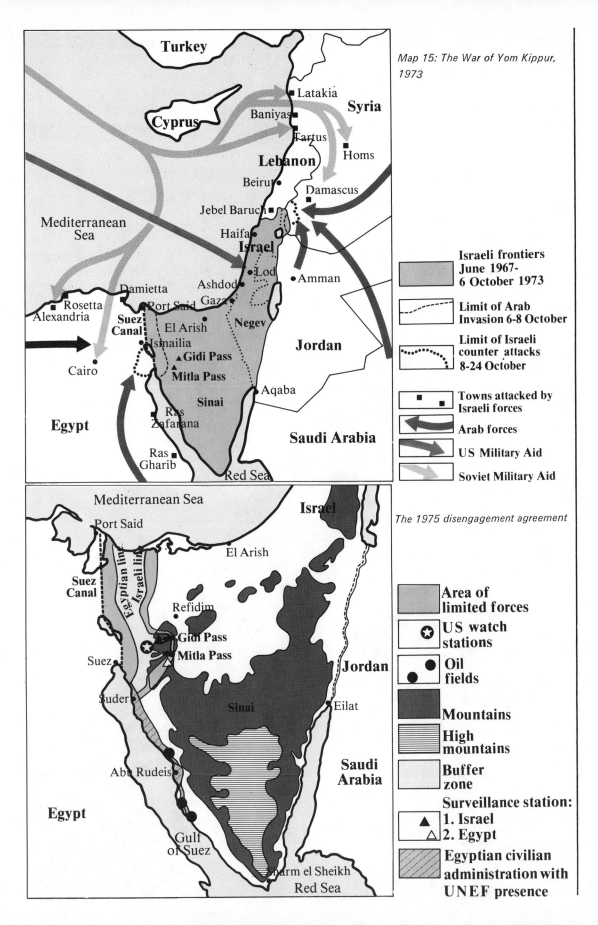

Map 15: The War of Yom Kippur, 1973

Israeli frontiers June 1967 - 6 October 1973

Limit of Arab Invasion 6-8 October

Limit of Israeli counter attacks 8-24 October

Towns attacked by Israeli forces

Arab forces

US Military Aid

Soviet Military Aid

The 1975 disengagement agreement

Area of limited forces

US watch stations

Oil fields

Mountains

High mountains

Buffer zone

Surveillance station:
1. Israel
2. Egypt

Egyptian civilian administration with UNEF presence

the Israelis had captured in 1967. It was clear to Defence Minister Moshe Dayan that Israel had to fight a war on two fronts. Her tactics were to deal first with the Syrian army which threatened Israeli settlements in North Galilee. Accordingly in the first part of the war the major Israeli effort was directed towards removing Syrian forces from the Golan Heights. This was achieved by 10 October but the drive towards Damascus was slowed down by the Arab counter attack launched by troops from Iraq and Jordan which joined the Syrian Forces. By the end of the war Israeli troops had occupied about 1500 square kilometres of Syrian territory.

The Israeli counter-offensive

Once the first attack had been repulsed in the north, the Israelis launched a counter-offensive against the Egyptians whom they had been containing on the Sinai front. The Egyptian forces had had considerable success in crossing the Suez Canal and establishing a line in some places as deep as 14 kilometres from the canal. After fierce tank battles in Sinai the Israelis forced a crossing into Egypt. They established a firm base on the west side of the river which placed them in a good position to attack Egyptian SAM missile sites and control the road to Cairo as well as the railway and parts of the west bank of the canal. However, Egyptian forces were able to retain narrow strips of land on the east bank.

SAM missile

King Hussein of Jordan makes a tour of the front line in Jordan

Russia and America intervene

During the war the Russians poured vast supplies of military equipment in to Egypt while the Americans gave military aid to Israel. However, by the tenth day of the war, the two super-powers were working for a cease-fire. Neither wished to become directly involved in a war with each other. Moreover the Russian leaders realised that the longer the war continued the more chance there was of a costly defeat for the Arabs. The American government was particularly influenced by the Arab policy of limiting oil production and banning the export of oil to America. The Russian and American leaders worked for a cease-fire with their respective client states and also in the Security Council of the United Nations. On 22 October after seventeen days of war a cease-fire was declared and after sporadic fighting a formal cease-fire agreement was eventually signed between the Egyptians and Israelis on 11 November at Kilometre 101 on the Cairo-Suez road.

The revival of the Arab fighting spirit

This war was very different from the Six Day War in 1967. The Arab forces not only benefited from attacking first but from their vastly improved military weapons and equipment. The Russians had installed about 130 launching sites for surface-to-air missiles along the Egyptian bank of the Suez Canal and these presented a formidable defence screen against Israeli penetration of Egyptian air space. The Soviet MiG aircraft were used more effectively by the Egyptians than in 1967 and the airfields were better protected. These factors ensured that Israel never achieved the full mastery of the air which had been so vital in the Six Day War.

The tanks and amphibious equipment from Russia also helped Egypt. The Soviet ground-to-ground missile equipment was a great asset to the Syrians in their initial attack in the Golan Heights and later in the defence of their land. In general, the Arab fighting men showed more heart and discipline compared with 1967. Not only were the troops in the field better trained and organised, but the Arab politicians showed a greater willingness to work together and a more realistic estimate of their military objectives. Their determination to ban oil exports was most effective in bringing pressure to bear on America. The limitation of their military objectives to recovering the occupied lands was far more realistic than the call in 1967 'to drive the Israelis into the sea'. Although the Arab forces suffered defeat in 1973, it was by no means as humiliating as in 1967. They had done much to win back their self-respect and restore their dignity. As *Al-Muharrir*, the Beirut daily newspaper, commented, 'The war marks the revival of the Arab fighting spirit'.

Wreckage of Syrian army vehicles on the road to Damascus, October 1973

PART 2

7 ISRAEL'S CHANGING BOUNDARIES

THE LANDS GAINED BY ISRAEL

Boundaries after the 1948-49 War

In 1947, when the UN voted for the partition of Palestine, they recommended that the Jewish State should be given approximately half of the land, to be located in the north west Mediterranean coast area and in the south east towards the Gulf of Aqaba. The proposed Arab state was to be assigned land along the south west coastal region and in north east. Jerusalem was to be in the Arab sector (see Map A).

The Arabs rejected partition and during the war which followed the Israelis captured some areas of the proposed Arab land. In fact by the end of the 1948-9 war the new State of Israel had acquired about 80 per cent of Palestine. This area was one third larger than the land allotted to the Jewish State by the 1947 UN partition plan. Most important to the Israelis, they took control of the western quarter of Jerusalem, their holy city (see Map B).

In 1950 the remaining Arab land on the west bank of the River Jordan around Jerusalem was annexed

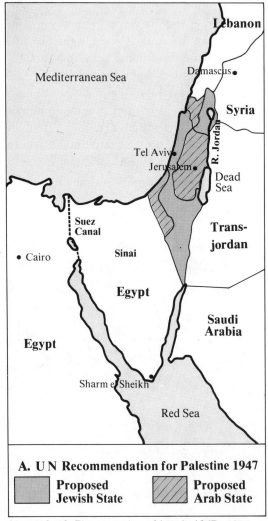

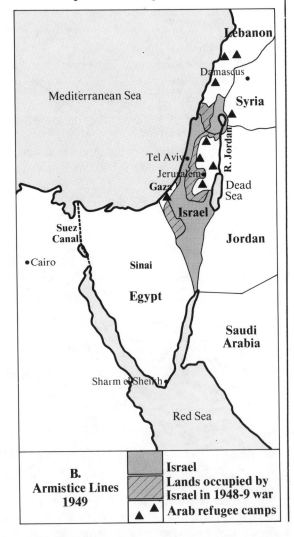

Maps 16–19: The expansion of Israel, 1947–1973

54

by King Abdullah of Transjordan. This Kingdom was now known as Jordan.

Gains after the Six Day War 1967

The Israeli gains of 1948–9 were valuable but the boundaries to the north-east and south-west of the Jewish State were not marked by obvious geographical features such as the River Jordan or the Gulf of Suez (see Map B). This made them difficult to defend. Furthermore, the Arabs still held part of Jerusalem.

By the end of the 1967 war, however, the Israelis had achieved a 'natural frontier' in these key regions. From Egypt, Israel acquired the Gaza Strip and Sinai, including the strong position of Sharm-el-Sheikh from which the Egyptians had blockaded the straits of Tiran. Israel also gained the Arab quarter of Jerusalem and the west bank area of the River Jordan from the Kingdom of Jordan. In the far north the Golan Heights were taken from Syria. Israel had increased her land three and a half times. Most important, however, she was now bordered directly by one canal (Suez), one river (Jordan), one mountain area (Golan), three seas (Mediterranean, Red and Dead Seas) and only three countries (Jordan, Syria and Lebanon). (See Map C.)

When the cease-fire was made at the end of the war of October 1973, Israeli forces also occupied an area on the Egyptian bank of the Suez Canal and part of Syria in the Golan region. By early February 1974, Israeli troops had evacuated all territory across the Suez Canal following the peace talks at Geneva.

In the interim peace agreement signed between Israel and Egypt in September 1975 Israel agreed to evacuate some 6250 square kilometres of occupied Sinai, including the Abu Rodeis oilfields and the

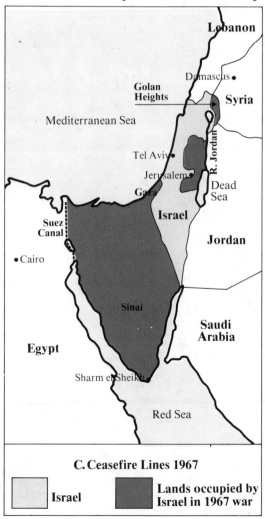

55

strategic Mitla and Giddi passes.

The Israeli dilemma

The Israelis have been faced with a dilemma. The more territory they have acquired the more Arabs they have living within their borders. For example, after the 1967 war there were over one million more Arabs in Israel. Most Israelis argue that their government cannot be expected to grant these Arabs full citizenship rights except under very stringent conditions. Those Arabs who make an application and meet the requirements will gain citizenship. However, many Israelis feel that if all the Arabs in Israel, now nearly one and a half million, were granted full civil and political rights, the whole idea of, and way of life in, that state would be destroyed. They say that Israel was established to provide a national home for the Jewish people whose ancestors had spent 2000 years scattered throughout the world. The Arabs within her borders have a different religion, way of life and allegiance.

The Arabs claim that appalling conditions exist in the occupied territories on the west bank of the Jordan and in the Gaza Strip. They also say that Israel has often deliberately destroyed Arab quarters in towns and cities like Jerusalem and Haifa and also wiped out whole Arab villages.

Orthodox Jews praying at the Wailing Wall, part of the western wall of Jerusalem

Most Israelis claim that the Arabs living in their country are treated reasonably in view of the circumstances. Most of the charges of brutality and repression are, they say, part of the Arab propaganda campaign against Israel. They claim that the strict but fair treatment of Arabs compares favourably with the way in which other Arab countries like Egypt have dealt with their Jewish communities. The fact that so many Arabs remain in Israel would suggest that most do not consider life there too severe or lacking in opportunities. Israelis admit that there has been some dislocation and resettlement of Arabs, but that this has been due to the destruction caused by war, various urban building schemes, the development of new agricultural villages and the creation of military bases on the borders of the country. Moreover, the Israelis claim that there has been no attempt to educate their youth to hate Arabs in the same way that children in many schools in Arab countries have been taught to hate Jews.

The issues of the expansion of Israel and the conditions of the Arabs living within her borders have been a cause of great bitterness between the Arab countries and Israel and are one of the major reasons for the repeated failure to secure a settlement of the Arab-Israeli dispute. You will learn more about the beliefs and attitudes of both sides from the following sources.

Source 22

A PURELY JEWISH STATE

Interviewer: 'Is there any possible way that Israel could absorb the huge numbers of Arabs whose territory it has gained control of now?'

Dayan: 'Economically we can; but I think that is not in accord with our aims in the future . . . we want to have a Jewish State. We can absorb them, but then it won't be the same country.'

Interviewer: 'And it is necessary to maintain this as a Jewish State and purely a Jewish State?'

Dayan: 'Absolutely — absolutely. We want a Jewish State like the French have a French State.'

(Moshe Dayan, Defence Minister of Israel, interviewed for C.B.S. *Face the Nation* T.V. programme, New York, June 1967)

A Syrian stamp commenting on the Palestine refugee problem

Source 23

THE FATE OF JEWS IN EGYPT

The founding of the Arab League in 1945 with headquarters in Cairo was the beginning of the end for the Egyptian Jewry, then numbering about 76 000. Fanatical organisations such as the 'Moslem Brotherhood', and Fascist organisations such as 'Young Egypt'

The Mosque of Omar, Jerusalem

began open incitement against the Jews. On the 2nd November 1945, a protest strike against the Balfour Declaration was proclaimed in Egypt for the first time. The demonstrators forced Jews to close their shops, many of which were looted. Synagogues were wrecked, and Scrolls of the Law were burnt in the streets.

On the day the State of Israel was proclaimed, the 14th May 1948, 2000 Jews were arrested in Egypt, hundreds more were placed under police surveillance on suspicion of 'activity directed against national security'.

Early in 1957, new rulings were made one after the other, making more and more Jews liable to arrest and expulsion. Citizenship was taken away from any Jew who had acquired it later than 1933, then from any Jew whom someone decided was a Zionist, then from any Jew who had acquired citizenship since 1900, then from any Jew who had ever been convicted for a crime, then from those who, though they had acquired citizenship before 1900, had not been in continuous residence since then.

Some Jews got out of the country and reached Israel, if not by the thousands by the hundreds. The rest still stayed on, helpless or fatalistic, or refusing to abandon home and property. But the Jewish community as such was already in a state of collapse. By 1960, synagogues were being closed down, some of them were converted into mosques and the rest were completely neglected. When

An anti-Jewish demonstration in Cairo, 1967

The illustration depicts Nasser as a new Hitler and comments on the fate of the Rabbi of Alexandria and other Egyptian Jews

the Jewish hospital was confiscated, the sick were put out into the street and the doctors and staff arrested. All the other community institutions—old age homes, orphanages, schools—were taken over, confiscated or closed down. Even the cemeteries were confiscated, sealed off, closed.

By June '67, there were probably no more than 2500 Jews left in Egypt. 1500 of them in Cairo and the rest in Alexandria. During May, Jews connected with or employed by public institutions had received letters sending them on vacation *sine die* and then follow-up letters dismissing them. Jewish bank accounts were frozen.

. . . The Jewish prisoners who had been arrested in Alexandria were brought to Cairo to join those in Abu Zaabal prison. On arrival the Rabbi of Alexandria was strung up to the prison gate in the form of one crucified and beaten unconscious.

What followed these arrests—a prolonged orgy of torture, part simply spiteful and part murderously sadistic . . . continued for many months thereafter.

The UN General Assembly passed a resolution in the Autumn of '68 requesting the Secretary General to send a commission to inquire into Israeli treatment of the Arab inhabitants of Israeli-occupied areas. Israel agreed to give official aid to such an inquiry, on condition that a similar inquiry be undertaken into the treatment of Jews in Arab countries. This was turned down.

(from *Arab Racialism* published by *The Israel Economist* in Jerusalem 1969)

A mathematics lesson in a Bedouin (Arab) village school near Haifa, Israel

THE DISPLACEMENT OF THE PALESTINIAN ARABS

Israel is a country which came into being by making another country cease to be. Israel is the replacement of a Middle Eastern country. Its people are recruited from a hundred different lands. The native people have been displaced and dispersed into a dozen lands. Its land is a land occupied but not owned, nor purchased, nor otherwise rightfully acquired by its present occupants. There is no other parallel to this situation anywhere else in the world today; and that is why the Arab-Israeli conflict cannot be understood in terms of other international situations . . .

That is why there is an Arab-Israeli conflict, and that is what the conflict is all about! When your reporters tell you: 'The Arab States do not recognise or accept Israel', they are reporting only half the truth: the other half of the truth is that the 'Israel' which the Arab States do not recognise or accept is a country whose very being has meant non-recognition and non-acceptance of the Arab people of Palestine. Arab non-recognition of Israel is no more than a passive retort to Israel's active and actualised non-recognition of Palestine.

(from L. Eaks, *Palestine: background to conflict* Petra Publishing Company, 1973)

SECOND CLASS CITIZENS

The Zionists consider the Arabs who reside in the occupied territories to be backward people, unworthy of equality of rights or of treatment, and undeserving of justice. They therefore should not have the same rights as the Jews either in education or in employment, and not even in law. The newly occupied lands after the 1967 aggression are experiencing a severe terrorist rule, while the Arabs who remained in Israel after 1948 have led the life of second class citizens and their lives have been exposed to many aspects of danger.

All methods of coercion are applied against the Arabs in the occupied terri-

Houses in the Arab quarter of Jerusalem

tories—including collective punishment. Arab prisoners are subjected to the most horrible tortures, both corporal and mental—not unlike those practised by the Nazis. The Zionists cold-bloodedly killed the Arab citizens in their villages, with a

An Egyptian stamp commenting on the plight of the Palestinian Arabs

view to spreading terror among the inhabitants and inducing them to escape from their homes and lands, thereby achieving one of two objectives: either to deport them or to subject them to the will of Zionist occupation.

The main purpose of mass extermination conducted by the Zionists is to wipe out all vestiges of Arab culture, expecting, in this manner, to efface everything connected with the Arabs in Palestine.

It is now the Israelis who lay down the study courses for Arab schools. These courses discard everything connected with the history of the country and its culture. The learning of Hebrew is obligatory for Arab pupils. The number of school-masters in Arab schools is very few, and the school equipment is deplorable. The level of education in Arab schools ends at a very low stage.

The Arabs are also barred from forming political parties or any other representative groups. The deportation of Arabs prominent in the domains of culture, politics, and religion has deprived the people of their leaders.

The Israeli army has exploited the emergency laws to take possession of Arab lands by force, on the pretext of their need for them for military purposes. By virtue of these pretexts, the army was able to come into possession of all Arab lands adjacent to the frontiers and erected thereon semi-military kibbutzim and frontier guard camps.

Terrorist groups of Israelis attacked Arab lands many times and occupied them, as had occurred in Hamdan village near Haifa, Kafr Saba, and Al-Tirah village.

The Arabs experienced serious racial discrimination in the field of employment. The majority of Arab workmen in Israel in 1963 . . . were suffering either from the low level of wages in comparison with the wages of Israelis, or from unemployment.

The Arab citizen residing in Israel is a bearer of a grade 'B' nationality card to show that he is a non-Jew Israeli subject, whereas, the Jewish citizen is a bearer of a different kind of card.

(from *Zionism—Racist Expansionist Movement,* published by The Arab League Office in Britain, 1969)

Source 26

WAKE UP

DO YOU KNOW
the facts about the torture and brutality inflicted upon political prisoners in Israel?

OR that Arabs are held in prison without charge?

OR that the great annual Moslem pilgrimage to Jerusalem has been stopped?

AND that nine million Arab Christians are denied access to Jerusalem?

DO YOU KNOW
that Arab land and property [are] seized without compensation?

OR that homes have been bulldozed with their occupants inside?

HAVE YOU LEARNT
about the contempt under Zionism for Christian and Moslem holy places, and the profanity and sacrilege now common in Jerusalem?

AND DO YOU CARE?

THEN JOIN THE JERUSALEM COMMITTEE.
(Published by the Jerusalem Committee in London, 1969)

Source 27

THE NATIONALITY LAW

To become an Israeli citizen an Arab must prove:

(*a*) he was born in the country;

(*b*) he has lived in Israeli-occupied territory three out of five years preceding the date of his application for citizenship;

(*c*) he is qualified for permanent residence;

(*d*) he is settled or intends to settle permanently in the country;

(*e*) he has sufficient knowledge of the Hebrew language.
(from *Israeli Government Yearbook, 1952*)

8 THE PALESTINE REFUGEES

THE REFUGEE PROBLEM

One of the bitterest, most tragic and insoluble issues dividing the Arab world from Israel is that of the Palestinian refugees.

In 1973 the Palestinian Arabs numbered approximately 3·3 million. Of these 1·4 million were living

An emergency camp in East Jordan for Palestinian refugees displaced during the 1967 war

in Israel. This group comprised those Arabs and their descendants who stayed in Israel after 1948 as well as those who since 1967 have lived under Israeli occupation on the west bank of the Jordan and the Gaza Strip. The rest of the Palestine Arabs—over one and a half million—live in exile. Most of them are in refugee camps. A few have been able to start a new life in Arab countries in the Middle East or have emigrated to Europe and South America.

There have been two mass exits of Arabs from Israel. The first occurred during the Arab-Israeli war of 1948–9 when about 750 000 Arabs fled from Israel; the second during the June war of 1967, when approximately 350 000 fled from the Gaza Strip and the west bank of the Jordan.

Refugee camps

The Arab refugee camps are located on the borders of Israel in Lebanon, Syria, Egypt and Jordan. Many people have lived in these camps for 25 years. It has proved almost impossible to lead any sort of civilised life. Most of the refugees cannot find employment. The vast majority are agricultural workers and are in direct competition with the under-employed farming population of those countries in which they are now living. The United Nations Organisation through its agency UNRWA (United Nations Relief and Works Agency) has maintained these camps and provided rations and some welfare services

An Emergency refugee camp for Palestinian Arabs in Syria

63

for the refugees. The numbers in the camps have grown because of the continual Arab exodus from Israel and the natural increase of population.

A barrier to peaceful negotiations

The refugee problem has caused tragic human misery (Source 28). It has also proved a constant barrier to successful peace negotiations between the Arab states and Israel. Except for about 40 000 refugees who returned under a family reunion scheme, Israel has resolutely refused to allow the refugees back.

Responsibility for the creation of the refugee problem has been hotly debated. The Arabs claim that the refugees were driven out by deliberate Jewish terrorism. In April 1948 Jewish guerrillas slaughtered 254 men, women and children at Deir Yassin, an Arab village to the west of Jerusalem. The Arabs claim that this and similar atrocities caused the Palestinian Arabs to flee in panic. On the other hand the Israelis claim that there would have been no refugees if the Arab states had not attacked Israel in May 1948. They assert that the Arabs were told by their leaders to leave in order to seek shelter in Arab lands and to clear the way for the combined Arab attack on Israel. The Israelis also say that the panic which contributed to the Arab exodus was largely caused by the violent radio propaganda of the Arab countries.

Palestinian refugee children eating a meal in a camp near Amman, Jordon

ONE IN THREE MILLION: THE STORY OF A PALESTINIAN

My name is Ghazi Daniel and I am 24 years old. I was born in Nazareth but today I am stateless.

In May 1948 when I was nine months old my family was forced to leave our beloved land. Father who was working in Haifa had to leave his job and Mother who was managing the shop we owned had to close it. Our house in Nazareth became deserted and our land, tilled by my uncles, was seized. We became destitute refugees in Lebanon.

As I was growing up I often felt furious. I wanted to know what had happened. My father tried to explain. He said that in 1948 Britain withdrew from Palestine. Massacres of our fellow Palestinians, like that of Deir Yassin, followed. In May 1948 the Zionists declared the establishment of the State of Israel. It was a state baptised in human blood. Like many of his country-men, my father was scared for our safety. Haifa was being shelled day and night from the neighbouring hills. Soldiers had found car batteries in our store. They said these could be used to detonate bombs and that my Father must be assisting the Palestinian Freedom Fighters. My parents decided to take my brothers, sisters and me to Lebanon. My father sold a piece of our land to pay for our food and lodging there until we could return to our home-land. The road to Lebanon was full of danger. We went by bus, by donkey and then on foot. Two kilometres before the border we had to crawl. Zionist snipers had decided if they could not shoot civilians at home they would shoot them when leaving their homes.

Unlike the childhood of others mine was full of sad memories. A few months after our arrival we were penniless and had to move into a refugee camp with 2000 other homeless Palestinians. It is beyond human endurance for a family of eleven to live in a small tent through all the seasons of the year on UNRWA rations. Fathers buried their children who died of malnutrition. Some buried their fathers who died of disease. On winter days we all crawled together to gain the warmth of humans which other humans had denied us.

In the UNRWA refugee camp school there were 50 students in my class. The class-room had a ceiling full of holes. We were left soaked every time it rained. We realised how crowded we were as we felt one another quiver when we prayed for our return. It was a hard life for my family. Our monthly rations lasted only a few days and our bellies were half empty all the time. My father finally found work as a carpenter. The meagre income was a little relief.

Our camp had no secondary school so I had to make a long journey each day to another camp. Later, to help ease the burden on my family I started to work, and, at the same time, attend an evening education course. In three years I earned my High School Certificate. However, I knew that this was the end of the road. University education was out of my reach.

The aggressive war of June 1967 was the second decisive landmark in my life. The new expansion of Israel and the new waves of refugees multiplied the tragedy many times. Perhaps, my thoughts will clarify to you those of my Palestinian sisters and brothers. I was faced with a dilemma. Standing at the crossroads I had to choose one path. I could obtain a job with a small salary and perhaps have a successful career. But should I seek a comfortable life and betray the hopes and dreams of my people? The two most cherished ideals of my people are to remain Palestinians and not be refugees. These can only be realised if we return to our country and our homes. I realised my dilemma was imaginary. I am left with no alternative but to fight our oppressor. This is why I have joined the Palestine National Liberation Movement. We shall fight for the Palestinians' return and for a new society in Palestine.

(This is an edited version of an account published by the Palestinian Liberation Organisation's Research Centre in Beirut, Lebanon, in 1972. Story narrated by Ghazi Daniel and written by Hani Faris.)

A WAR OF WORDS

The Arabs claim that Israel has made certain the refugees would have little to come back to. Many Arab villages and Arab quarters in towns and cities have been destroyed. Israel counters by saying that most of the destruction of Arab property occurred either as a result of the war of 1948–9 or because of urban rebuilding schemes. Israel claims that she has been prepared to consider the question of compensation for Arab losses. However, Israeli leaders have made it clear that any sum arrived at for compensation would have to take into account the effect of the Arab boycott of Israeli goods and Israel's heavy military expenditure which they claim is forced upon her by Arab hostility.

The Arabs assert that the Palestinian Arabs have a right to live in their homeland and that repatriation is the only solution to the problem. The declared policy of the Arab states is to work to restore this right to the refugees (Source 29). Since 1950 the Israelis have consistently resisted all schemes of repatriation; they claim that it would be very difficult to make room for over a million returning Arabs. Their primary duty is to encourage immigration of Jews into Israel. Moreover the Arabs who returned would not only create security problems for Israel but would not be likely to live in harmony with Jews. The Israelis claim that no attempt has been made by the Arab states—particularly the oil-rich countries of Kuwait and Saudi Arabia—to provide food and shelter for their Arab brothers in the refugee camps. This contrasts with the efforts of Jews all over the world, but particularly in Britain and the USA who have raised hundreds of millions of pounds to help settle their own people in Israel.

Abba Eban, Israeli Foreign Minister, 1972

The Israelis also point out that the Arab governments have steadfastly refused to allow the refugees to take part in the economic and social life of their countries. The Israelis claim that the refugees have not been absorbed into the Arab community for political reasons. The refugees can be used as a bargaining point against Israel in negotiations. They provide a source of sympathy for the Arab cause and the discontented refugees can be exploited to undertake terrorist raids against Israel.

Source 29

AN EXTRACT FROM THE SPEECH OF ABBA EBAN, CHIEF ISRAELI REPRESENTATIVE TO THE UNITED NATIONS, IN NEW YORK ON 17 NOVEMBER 1958

. . . The perpetuation of this refugee problem is an unnatural event, running against the whole course of experience and precedent. Since the end of the Second World War problems affecting forty million refugees have confronted governments in various parts of the world. In no case, except that of the Arab refugees, amounting to less than two per cent of the whole, has the international community shown constant responsibility and provided lavish aid. In every other case a solution has been found by the integration of refugees into their host countries . . . In this case alone has integration been obstructed.

The paradox is the more astonishing when we reflect that the kinship of language, religion, social background and national sentiment existing between the Arab refugees and their Arab host countries has been at least as intimate as those existing between any other host countries and any other refugee groups.

. . . It is painfully evident that this refugee problem has been artificially maintained for political motives against all the economic, social and cultural forces which, had they been allowed free play, would have brought about a solution.

Recent years have witnessed a great expansion of economic potentialities in the Middle East. The revenues of the oil-bearing countries have opened up great opportunities of work and development, into which the refugees by virtue of their linguistic and national background could fit without any sense of dislocation. The expansion in the areas of Arab sovereignty has also created opportunities of employment which did not exist in the days of colonial rule. There cannot be any doubt that if free movement had been granted to the refugees there would have been a spontaneous absorption of thousands of them into these expanded Arab economies. It is precisely this that Arab governments have obstructed.

. . . There has, of course, been some movement of refugees into the new labour opportunities of the region. But these potentialities can only be fully realised if political resistance to integration is overcome. There are broad opportunities in the Arab world for refugees to build new lives; but the governments concerned have so far sought to debar refugees from using them.

. . . The failure or refusal of Arab governments to achieve a permanent economic integration of refugees in their huge lands appears all the more remarkable when we contrast it with the achievements of other countries when confronted by the challenge and opportunity of absorbing their kinsmen into their midst. Israel with her small territory, her meagre water resources and her hard-pressed finances, has found homes, work and citizenship in the past ten years for nearly a million new-comers arriving in destitution no less acute than those of Arab refugees. These refugees from Arab lands left their homes, property and jobs behind. Their standards of physique and nutrition were in many cases pathetically low. They have had to undergo processes of adaptation to a social, linguistic and national ethos far removed from any that they had known before. Thus, integration in this case has been far more arduous than it would be for Arab refugees in Arab lands, where no such differences exist between the society and culture of the host country and those with which the refugees are already familiar. If Israel in these conditions could assimilate nearly one million refugees—450 000 of them from Arab lands—how much more easily could the vast Arab world find a home for a similar number of Arab refugees, if only the same impulse of kinship asserted itself.

. . . In the light of these experiences it cannot be doubted that Arab governments have been determined that the refugees shall remain refugees; and that the aim of wrecking any alternative to 'repatriation' has been pursued by these governments with an ingenuity worthy of a better cause. With an international agency working for integration; with millions of dollars expended every year to move refugees away from a life of dependence, the Arab governments have brought us to a point where there are more refugees on United Nations rolls than ever before.

(from W. Laqueur, *The Israel-Arab Reader*)

AN INSOLUBLE PROBLEM?

The Palestine refugees have presented a challenge to both the Israelis and the Arabs. Neither has been able to find a solution. So far the efforts of the United Nations to find a satisfactory answer have come to nothing. It seems likely that the problem will remain until there is a general peace in the Middle East. Meanwhile many Palestinian Arabs still live in camps. It is not surprising that they have become increasingly resentful of their wretched lives and expectations.

9 PALESTINE LIBERATION MOVEMENTS

In May 1964 the Palestine Liberation Organisation (PLO) was officially formed. Its spokesman was

Two Palestinian guerrilla snipers in camouflage prepare to go into action in the Jordon valley

Ahmed Shukairy, who had served earlier as an Arab representative at the United Nations. Shukairy and his committee drew up their manifesto 'The Palestine National Covenant' (Source 30). The main aim was to work for the return of the Palestinian Arabs to their homeland.

The PLO claimed that the Arab people of Palestine were the victims of grave injustice. They argued that there was no justification for the Jewish claim to Palestine since in international law possession of a territory is lost after a hundred years of non-possession. The Jewish claim was resurrected nearly 2000 years after their dispersal from the area. The resolution of the United Nations in 1947 which gave the Jews part of Palestine was unjust. The UN was largely influenced by the sufferings that the Jews had undergone in Germany under Hitler and earlier in Poland and Russia. The Arabs say they had been made to pay for the wrongs done in Europe to the Jews.

Although the PLO was recognised by the Arab governments and received some support from them it was the overwhelming Arab defeat in the 1967 war which sparked the movement into vigorous activity. It became clear to most members that their future lay in their own hands. The failure of the leaders and armies of the Arab countries in the June war showed that even if their full support was forthcoming, it was not likely to be effective. The United Nations and the world powers had also failed to help them regain their homeland. Moreover, all the land in Palestine which had remained in Arab hands after 1948 was lost. The Gaza Strip and all the territory on the west bank of the River Jordan which had been part of the Kingdom of Jordan since 1950 was lost to the Israelis during the war.

The refugees in the camps on the borders of Israel, swelled by the Arab exodus of 1967, were becoming increasingly embittered. Many joined the various Palestinian organisations. Arabs from inside and outside the camps became active members of the Palestine Freedom Fighters (Source 31).

Source 30

AN EXTRACT FROM
THE PALESTINE NATIONAL
COVENANT
MAY 1964

Article 1. Palestine is an Arab homeland bound by strong Arab National ties to the rest of the Arab Countries and which together form the large Arab Homeland.

Article 2. Palestine with its boundaries at the time of the British Mandate is a regional indivisible unit.

Article 3. The Palestinian Arab people has the legitimate right to its homeland and is an inseparable part of the Arab Nation. It shares the sufferings and inspirations of The Arab Nation, and its struggle for freedom, sovereignty, progress and unity.

[Articles 4–5 are omitted]

Article 6. The Palestinians are those Arab citizens who were living normally in Palestine up to 1947, whether they remained or were expelled. Every child who was born to a Palestinian parent after this date whether in Palestine or outside is a Palestinian.

Article 7. Jews of Palestinian origin are considered Palestinians if they are willing to live peacefully and loyally in Palestine.

Article 8. Bringing up Palestinian youth in an Arab nationalist manner is a fundamental national duty. All means of guidance, education and enlightenment should be utilized to introduce the youth to its homeland in a deep spiritual way that will constantly and firmly bind them together.

[Articles 9–11 are omitted]

Article 12. Arab unity and the liberation of Palestine are two complementary goals; each prepares for the attainment of the other. Arab unity leads to the liberation of Palestine, and the liberation of Palestine leads to Arab unity. Working for both must go side by side.

Source 31

A NATION OF BEGGARS?

'For twenty years our people have been waiting for a just solution of the Palestine Problem,' wrote a graduate student at the American University of Beirut in a letter to his parents. 'All that we got was charity and humiliation while others continue to live in our homes. I refuse to remain a refugee. I have decided to join the freedom fighters and I ask for your blessings.'

Meanwhile, in a refugee camp near Amman, Jordan, the mother of a freedom fighter who died in action on occupied Palestinian soil says: 'I am proud that he did not die in this camp. The foreign press comes here and takes our pictures standing in queues to obtain food rations. They publish these photographs giving the impression that we are a 'nation of beggars'. This is no life. I am proud of having sent my second son to replace the first; and I am already preparing my eight-year old boy for the day when he can fight for liberation too.'

(from a pamphlet published by the Palestine National Liberation Movement in Britain in 1969)

Refugees queuing for food in a camp in Jordan, November 1967

AL-FATAH

The group called the Palestine National Liberation Movement has played an important part in the development of the Palestinian struggle. This group, led by Yasser Arafat, is often known by its Arab name—Al-Fatah. (See biography, page 71.)

Its basic aims are to restore the Palestinian Arabs to their homeland and to create a state in Palestine in which all people will have equal rights irrespective of their race and religion. Al-Fatah led the way by adopting guerrilla tactics against Israel. In 1964 its military wing, Al-Assifa, made its first raid into Israeli territory.

Al-Assifa took part in the fighting in the west bank sector during the June war of 1967. When the war was over the group pulled back to the east bank and formed a base at Karameh in the Jordan Valley. Frequent guerrilla raids were organised across the border into Israel. In March 1968 the Israelis launched a full scale attack which destroyed Karameh. However, with support from the regular Jordanian army, the men of Al-Assifa repulsed the Israelis. Gradually Al-Assifa increased its membership and established itself as the most powerful and influential resistance group.

ARAB TERRORISTS

In 1968 Yasser Arafat tried to coordinate the commando activities of the various groups. However, some organisations refused to cooperate, including the Popular Democratic Front for the Liberation of

BIOGRAPHY: YASSER ARAFAT

Early life

Arafat was born in Jerusalem in 1928. In his 'teens he became a guerrilla fighter during the time of the British mandate. He supplied detachments of the Arab forces with arms during the 1948–9 Arab-Israeli war. After the war he lived for a time in a refugee camp in Gaza. Later he attended Cairo University where, with his close friend Kalah Khalaf, he formed his first political movement—a Palestinian students' organisation. In 1952 Arafat set up a guerrilla group to launch raids into Israel. When the Suez war came in 1956 he served as an engineer in the Egyptian army.

Founder of Al-Fatah

In 1958 he founded a group called Al-Fatah which means 'victory'. The name also represents the initials of Harakat Al-Tahriv Al-Falistini (the Palestine Liberation Movement) read backwards. At this time the Algerian government allowed Al-Fatah to establish a secret office in their country and Syria gave the movement some support.

From 1965 to 1967 periodic guerrilla attacks on Israel were organised. The Arab defeat in the 1967 war convinced Arafat and his colleagues that they should become full time revolutionaries. In September 1967 Yasser Arafat had his first meeting with President Nasser, who promised military supplies. President Aref of Iraq gave him financial backing and King Feisal of Saudi Arabia permitted Al-Fatah to collect subscriptions in his country for the Palestine families of guerrillas who had been wounded and killed.

1968—a successful year

1968 was a successful year for Arafat. In the battle of Karameh in the Jordan valley, Al-Fatah, with assistance from the Jordanian Army, strongly resisted the attack of Israeli forces. Thousands of new members, delighted with this stand, flocked to Al-Fatah. Arafat was appointed Chairman of the Palestine Liberation Movement. In July 1968 he was in Russia when President Nasser was on a visit there. It is reported that Nasser presented him to the Soviet officials and told them with a grin, 'This is the Palestinian problem—deal with him'. In October Al-Fatah announced its aim of a democratic, secular state in Palestine with equal rights for Jews, Muslims and Christians. Guerrilla raids on Israel continued.

The Palestinian cause in the 1970s

The failure of the PLO guerrillas in Jordan in 1970 was a serious drawback for Arafat. Two of his closest colleagues were captured. However, President Nasser persuaded King Hussein to release them. Since 1970 Al-Fatah has received military aid from both China and Russia. The Soviet Union, in particular, has expressed support for the creation of a Palestinian state in the Israeli-occupied West Bank. Also at a summit conference of Arab leaders in 1973 support was given to the formation of a Palestinian state between Israel and Jordan. The Arab states, with the exception of Jordan, recognised the PLO as the sole representative of the Palestinian people. There is no doubt of the popularity of Arafat and the PLO amongst the Arab people in refugee camps and in the Arab states in general. Nevertheless, he has not been able to secure the support of all the Palestine Liberation groups. It is said that Arafat is particularly critical of the terrorist attacks on civilian targets of some of these groups.

Palestine (PDFLP). This group had taken the lead in attacking Israeli airports and towns, as well as undertaking raids on Israeli outposts.

The wreckage of an aircraft after an Israeli commando raid on Beirut airport, December 1968

The Arab terrorists were seen by most of their people as heroic freedom fighters aiming to regain their homeland, whereas the Israelis regarded them as agents of murder and sabotage. Letter bombs and other forms of attack on individuals with Jewish connections were also employed (Source 32). How far these activities gained sympathy for the Palestinian cause remains to be seen.

The Palestinian Liberation Movement has not made the progress for which it hoped. The guerrilla raids into Israel have spread terror and harassment but no military victory has been achieved. Israel has not given in to Arab demands. Moreover, the various movements working for the recovery of Palestine are divided in their aims and methods. Some extremists aim to destroy Israel and replace the Jews by Arabs in Palestine. Many support the aims of Al-Fatah. Strong support has developed for an independent state on the west bank of the Jordan. Some groups believe only in peaceful means. Most employ militant methods. However, some militant groups draw a distinction between raids on Israeli military targets and attacks on civilians.

Jewish children without home or a mother after an Arab guerrilla bomb attack, February 1970

Source 32

A BRUTAL CRIME

Words such as 'outrage' and 'horror' have been so loosely used that they seem inadequate when applied to the attempted assassination of Mr Joseph Sieff [Managing Director of Marks and Spencer]. An outrage it was indeed. Few events should be more capable of arousing in us feelings of rage and horror, more capable of alerting us to the decay of the social restraints on anarchy we take for granted, than an open unashamed murderous attack on a private citizen in his own home purely because of his political and religious views. Here it is unimportant that Mr Sieff is a public benefactor whose commercial skills have obtained for the British people, at all levels, greater benefits than were ever provided by a government. His prominence merely gives the crime an interest which—alas—similar atrocities in Northern Ireland no longer wring from our blunted sensibilities.

Of his attackers, the Popular Front for the Liberation of Palestine, what can be said? Brutal, unfeeling, ruthless, employing barbarities which no ordinary thug, uncorrupted by devotion to a cause, would ever contemplate, asserting the doctrine that the unfulfilled rights of the Palestinian Arabs justify atrocities everywhere in the world—a recipe for endless, universal turmoil—they are a modern politicised version of the Barbary pirates. Sooner or later, if a Geneva peace solution does not persuade them to disband, the international community must root them out.

(from *The Daily Telegraph*, 2 January 1974)

President Nasser with Yasser Arafat and King Hussein of Jordan

RELATIONSHIPS WITH ARAB GOVERNMENTS

The Communist PDFLP differs from Al-Fatah in its philosophy and tactics. In particular, it is hostile to most governments of the Arab states. The members of these governments, they claim, are primarily concerned with their own class and national interests and are not sympathetic to the Palestinians. The PDFLP believes that success lies with the union of peoples rather than rulers.

The Palestine Liberation Movement has frequently been in dispute with the various Arab governments. There was a civil war in Jordan in September 1970 between King Hussein and the Palestinian guerrillas. Jordan has the largest number of Palestinian exiles of any Arab state. It was used as a base by many Palestine organisations. King Hussein became increasingly hostile to their activities. He objected to their raids against Israel after the cease-fire between Israel and the Arab states in August 1970 and the hijacking of planes. A struggle for power broke out but the Jordan army remained loyal and the attempted take-over failed. This was another setback for the Palestinian Movement.

10 THE UNITED NATIONS ORGANISATION AND THE ARAB-ISRAELI CONFLICT

The United Nations Organisation was established with many aims in view. The most important of these was to maintain world peace. Another was to give special assistance to disadvantaged groups of people in the world. The Arab-Israeli dispute has presented the United Nations with a series of problems which have proved very difficult to solve.

UN headquarters building in New York

THE PALESTINE PARTITION PLAN, 1947

In 1947 the British government referred the problem of Palestine to the United Nations. A special committee on Palestine (UNSCOP) was set up and its report and recommendations were published in

August 1947. On 29 November 1947, the UN Assembly endorsed the partition plan by which Palestine was to be divided into Arab and Jewish states. Neither Britain nor the Arabs accepted this plan but in May 1948 the new country, Israel, was proclaimed. Later Israel became a member of the United Nations.

Stamp commemorating the work of the United Nations for human rights

Since the early days of the new state, the United Nations has been faced with many problems, both in the General Assembly and the Security Council, and in its specialised agencies like the International Labour Organisation (ILO), the World Health Organisation (WHO) and the United Nations Educational, Scientific and Cultural Organisation (UNESCO).

THE REFUGEE PROBLEM

In response to the plight of the refugees who had fled from Palestine during the 1948–9 war, the UN set up a Relief and Works Agency (UNRWA). Camps were established in Egypt, Syria, Lebanon and Jordan. Help was given to the refugees in the form of food, shelter, schools and medical services. By May 1967, before the Six Day War caused a new exodus, the number of refugees and their descendants

UNRWA nutrition clinic in an emergency refugee camp in East Jordan; the clinic was set up to treat children suffering from undernourishment and dehydration after gastro-enteritis

75

registered with UNRWA was 1 345 000. Of these 723 000 were in Jordan, 317 000 in Gaza, 161 000 in Lebanon and 144 000 in Syria. UNRWA continued its work in camps in Gaza and the west bank of the Jordan when these areas fell under Israeli occupation following the 1967 war (Source 33). UNRWA has done much to lessen the suffering of many refugees throughout its twenty-five years' existence. However, since December 1948 numerous UN resolutions recognising the rights of Palestinian refugees to repatriation and compensation have in practice been ignored by Israel.

A refugee camp in Syria

THE WORK OF UNRWA IN THE GAZA REFUGEE CAMPS, 1971

These people have to rely on the United Nations Relief and Works Agency for their food sustenance, because they are unable to add or supplement the monthly food rations they receive from UNRWA.

A person on the UNRWA rations list receives 10 kilos of flour, 500 grams of rice, 500 grams of sugar, and two cups of soybean oil monthly. During the winter months UNRWA provides one litre of kerosene for each ration card holder, each month. UNRWA would also supplement these rations with other edible goods they might receive. Children between the ages of 6–10 receive 500 grams of meat to supplement their monthly diet. These rations provide for an average calorie intake of 1500 calories per day. Only about two-thirds of the refugees receive this monthly allocation of rations from UNRWA. The reason for this is that UNRWA has placed a ceiling on the number of people who can receive rations, because their funds are inadequate to provide for everyone.

Medical treatment provided by UNRWA is good under the existing conditions but there are too few doctors for the number of people living in Gaza. In Gaza there are about thirty doctors for 400 000 people. The average case load for a doctor will vary from 125 to 150 cases per day, which places a tremendous strain on them. Most of the medical cases will deal with dehydration, nutritional problems and infections.

(from an article by R. Ambling in the *Daily Star* of Beirut, Lebanon, 28 March 1971)

Danish and Canadian UN officers escorted by Israeli troops inspect the cease-fire line, June 1967

UN PEACE-KEEPING MISSIONS

The UN's peace-keeping missions have hardly been more successful. In spite of two truces in 1948, it was not until January 1949 that an armistice was signed. It was soon obvious that this would not be followed by a lasting peace. In December 1949 the UN Assembly passed a resolution once more recommending a permanent international administration in the divided city of Jerusalem, but the scheme failed completely. Israel not only proclaimed Jerusalem as its capital city, but moved its parliament there. In 1953 King Abdullah of Jordan made Jerusalem his second capital. In 1967 Israeli troops captured the Arab sector of the city in the Six Day War and incorporated it into Israel.

In spite of the 1949 armistice, Egypt maintained a strict blockade in the Suez Canal of Israeli ships, and ships carrying goods to Israel, ignoring also a UN resolution of September 1951. When the UN General Assembly met on 1 November 1956, John Foster Dulles of the USA secured the passing of a draft resolution calling for a cease-fire after the outbreak of war in October. It is perhaps not surprising that this cease-fire was more effective than some. However, the UN Emergency Force (UNEF), organised to supervise the cease-fire, was stationed only on the Egyptian side of the Sinai border; the Israelis refused to allow the forces on their side.

Even on the Egyptian side the UN forces did not seem to have much authority. When in May 1967 President Nasser asked them to leave, UN Secretary General U Thant agreed. Abba Eban, a prominent Israeli statesman, has claimed that it was this action of the UN, together with its failure to act firmly in other matters, which contributed to the development of the 1967 crisis.

When the war ended on 10 June, efforts were made to secure a basis for negotiations. In November 1967 a British sponsored resolution (242) was approved by the Security Council (Source 34). In particular it called for the withdrawal of Israeli forces from territories occupied in the recent conflict, and for the recognition by all States in the area of each other's sovereignty. For seventeen months Dr Gunnar Jarring of Sweden, acting as UN mediator, tried to secure the agreement of the Arab States and Israel to the resolution. But there seemed no answer to the fact that the Arabs insisted that Israel withdraw her forces from the territories occupied in 1967 *before* negotiations could begin, while the Israelis demanded that the Arabs should negotiate with them *before* they withdraw: they saw the extent of their withdrawal as a matter for negotiation.

President Nasser and U Thant discussing the Middle East situation with General Rikhye, Commander of the UN Emergency Force which was withdrawn from Egypt, May 1967

Dr Henry Kissinger with Dr Kurt Waldheim

On 22 October 1973, after the fourth Arab-Israeli War, the UN Security Council adopted resolution 338 (Source 35) calling for a cease-fire, and a UN peace-keeping force was sent to the Suez area to supervise the cease-fire. The armistice agreement was signed on 11 November 1973. This was the first joint document which the two sides had signed since 1949. It was based on a letter sent by Dr Kissinger, US Secretary of State, to the UN Secretary General, Dr Kurt Waldheim, on 9 November, 1973.

In December 1973 the Peace Conference began its sessions in Geneva. Dr Kissinger of the USA and

Mr Gromyko, the Russian foreign minister, acted as co-chairmen of the Conference although a delegation from the UN, headed by Dr Waldheim, was present. This meeting was the first time that Arabs and Israelis had sat together at a peace conference. As a result of their deliberations Israel and Egypt agreed to the disengagement of their forces along the Suez Canal and in 1975 the Canal was re-opened to shipping.

Israeli troops handing over a 29 km stretch of the Suez-Cairo road to UN Emergency Forces during the first phase of the disengagement agreement, June 1974

Source 34

AN EXTRACT FROM SECURITY COUNCIL RESOLUTION 242 ON THE MIDDLE EAST 22 NOVEMBER 1967

The Security Council

1. Affirms that the fulfilment of Charter principles requires the establishment of a just and lasting peace in the Middle East which should include the application of both the following principles:

   (i) Withdrawal of Israeli armed forces from territories of recent conflict;

   (ii) Termination of all claims or states of belligerency and respect for and acknowledgement of the sovereignty, territorial integrity and political independence of every state in the area and their right to live in peace within secure and recognised boundaries free from threats or acts of force;

2. Affirms further the necessity

   (a) For guaranteeing freedom of navigation through international waterways in the area;

   (b) For achieving a just settlement of the refugee problem;

   (c) For guaranteeing the territorial inviolability and political independence of every state in the area, through measures including the establishment of demilitarized zones.

   (from W. Laqueur, *The Israel-Arab Reader*)

Source 35

UN SECURITY COUNCIL RESOLUTION 338 22 OCTOBER 1973

The Security Council

1. Calls upon all parties to the present fighting to cease all firing and terminate all military activity immediately, no later than 12 hours after the moment

of the adoption of this decision, in the positions they now occupy:

2. Calls upon the parties concerned to start immediately after the ceasefire the implementation of Security Council Resolution 242 (1967) in all of its parts:

3. Decides that, immediately and concur-rently with the cease-fire, negotiations start between the parties concerned under appropriate auspices aimed at establishing a just and durable peace in the Middle East.

(from *The Guardian,* 21 December 1973)

Yasser Arafat states the PLO case at the United Nations in New York, November 1974

SHOULD ISRAEL REMAIN A MEMBER OF THE UN?

The reason for UN failure in the Middle East is a much debated matter, but most Arabs regard it as the fault of Israel for not acting upon UN resolutions. Because Israel·has repeatedly ignored the UN, the Arabs and particularly the Palestinians, argue that she should no longer remain a member. They have campaigned for her expulsion in the General Assembly in New York and, since the 1967 war, in some of the specialised agencies. For example, in the WHO the Israelis are accused of damaging the physical and mental health of people in the occupied Arab territories. In the International Labour Organisation they are charged with discriminating against Arab workers. (For the Arab view, see Source 36.)

Source 36

As with South Africa, it can be strongly argued that the Government of Israel not only merits expulsion in the light of her refusal to observe the UN Charter and Resolution, but neither does Israel's Government represent all the people of Palestine. Having recognised the Palestinian people's rights in Palestine, the

United Nations can hardly assert that the present Government of Israel is the legitimate representative of Palestine at the United Nations. The question of Israel's and South Africa's representation at the United Nations is not a question of the right of these countries to be represented (as was the case enforced by the United States over China, North Vietnam and North Korea) but a matter of who is to represent these countries, Governments based on minorities, or the disenfranchisement of racial and religious communities, must surely come under the strictest review.

(from the Editorial in *Free Palestine* August/September 1975)

11 THE SUPER POWERS AND THE ARAB-ISRAELI DISPUTE

The Arab-Israeli dispute is an issue of concern not only to the people and governments of the Middle East. It also involves the rival countries of the United States of America and Russia. The two super-powers have exercised considerable influence on the course of the conflict and on the prospects of a permanent peace settlement.

"Double, Double . . ."

A Punch cartoon of 1 November 1967, commenting on American and Russian arms supplies to the Middle East

RUSSIAN INVOLVEMENT

Russia and Nasser's Egypt

The Russian interests in the Middle East developed in the years after 1945. Her influence was firmly established in Egypt by 1956. The Egyptians were seeking economic, military and diplomatic assistance. In particular a loan was needed to build the Aswan Dam. In 1955 President Nasser secured military equipment from Communist Czechoslovakia. In 1956 Russia gave support to Nasser when the Suez Canal was nationalised and promised him financial help when the World Bank refused to grant a loan for the Dam project. During the Suez War of 1956 Russia gave diplomatic support to Egypt and bitterly denounced the intervention of British and French forces (Source 37).

Russian warship on the move from the Black Sea to the Mediterranean

In the years after 1956 Russia consolidated her influence in Egypt. Specialists in economic affairs came to advise the Egyptians and help was given with the Hellwan steel works project. Trade was developed between the two countries and by 1967 half Egypt's exports went to Russia. The Egyptian armed forces were improved by Russian military advice and equipment. After the 1967 Arab-Israeli war Russia gradually replaced the Egyptian aircraft, tanks and guns which had been destroyed or abandoned. In 1970 a network of missile launching sites was set up to protect the Cairo-Alexandria region from Israeli air raids. By December 1970 the Egyptian air defence system extended to the Suez Canal.

The Israeli army advances near Suez

In fifteen years the Russians had established a strong influence in Egypt, by now one of the most important Arab countries. Russia had gained facilities for her Mediterranean fleet at Alexandria harbour and Cairo Airport provided a base for her Middle East reconnaissance aircraft.

Yet Russian influence over Egypt still had its limitations. Members of the Egyptian Communist Party had little success in gaining influential positions in the government. There is also evidence to suggest that the Russians did not approve of the provocative Egyptian actions which led to the Six Day War in 1967. At this stage, however, links between the two governments were still strong enough for Russia to come out publicly in support of Egypt (Source 38).

Source 37

HANDS OFF EGYPT

The government of the Soviet Union thinks that, in the interests of preserving peace and order in the region of the Near and Middle East, the United Nations must take immediate steps for the cessation of aggressive actions towards Egypt by France and England and an immediate withdrawal of the interventionist troops from the territory of Egypt. In connection with the sabotage by England and France in the Security Council, the responsibility for the solution of this problem falls now upon the extraordinary session of the General Assembly of the UN, called by the decision of the majority of the Security Council members.

. . . The Anglo-French colonisers do not conceal the fact that in committing aggression against Egypt they pursue much fuller aims. Their schemes are not limited to attempts to seize the Suez Canal and to occupy Egyptian territory. It is a matter of direct threat to all Arab states that strive to strengthen their national independence. Moreover, the imperialist spheres of England and France defy all the peoples of the East who make a stand for their national independence and sovereignty. These circles plan to intimidate the freedom-loving peoples of Asia and Africa and to force them by fire and sword to retreat in the sacred combat for independence and peace.

(from the Russian newspaper *Pravda*, 2 November 1956)

Source 38

PERFIDY AND AGGRESSION

The Security Council debates showed up the broad imperialist conspiracy against the Arab states and peoples of the Middle East. It was proved that the Israeli aggression was not an accidental thing, nor the result of any mistake or misunderstanding. No, it was a carefully plotted imperialist provocation, the timing of which was planned on all sides. This aggression was to secure political changes in the Middle East in the interest of imperialism, notably American imperialism, to alter the 'balance of strength' in the area. Its purpose was to undermine the Arab national liberation movement, to weaken the progressive regimes in Egypt, Syria and other Arab countries. Israel acted as the instrument of more powerful imperialist states, and above all the US.

The Israeli army was built up and trained with the help of the imperialist Western powers. Tel Aviv was given every protection and encouragement, particularly in Washington, to prepare it for aggression against the Arab States.

The peoples of Egypt and other Arab countries have scored historic victories in these past years in their struggle to attain national independence and freedom. Important social restructuring and reform in the interests of the working masses has been carried out in these countries. The imperialists could not stomach the fact that in this struggle the Arab peoples lean on the friendship and support of the Soviet Union and other socialist states.

(from the Russian magazine, *New Times*, 28 June 1967. This article was written by N. T. Fedorenko, the Russian delegate to the United Nations.)

Russia and Sadat's Egypt

After Nasser's death in 1970 Russia's relationship with Egypt deteriorated. During the Yom Kippur War of 1973, Russia and America co-operated to enforce a cease-fire between Arabs and Israelis. By April 1974 an open breach appeared between Russia and Egypt. President Sadat announced that Egypt would follow a 'new' foreign policy based on neutrality towards super-powers Russia and America (Source 39). In March 1976 Sadat ended the 1971 Treaty of Friendship with Russia and withdrew naval facilities for Soviet warships at Egyptian ports. Egypt was no longer a 'client state' of Russia.

Dr Henry Kissinger touching glasses with President Sadat of Egypt after a meeting in Salzburg, Austria, January 1975

Source 39

PRESIDENT SADAT OUTLINES EGYPT'S ATTITUDE TO AMERICA AND RUSSIA, APRIL 1974

In a speech on April 18 . . . President Sadat stressed that Egypt's foreign policy would be based on non-alignment and 'positive neutrality' between the two super-powers, declaring in this connection: 'We will not befriend America at the expense of the Soviet Union and we will not befriend the Soviet Union at the expense of America; whoever offers us the hand of friendship, we offer him the hand of friendship in return'. In the course of his speech President Sadat announced that Egypt would end its exclusive reliance on Soviet arms supplies and would seek arms from other sources as well as from the USSR. This decision, he intimated, had been made after the Soviet Union had failed for the last six months to act on his requests for arms deliveries. In this period, said President Sadat, four messages had been sent to Moscow, but he had received only two replies saying that the requests were being studied.

In an interview to journalists on April 21 President Sadat said that Egypt had decided to cease relying on the Soviet Union as an exclusive source of arms supplies because the USSR had used these supplies as an 'instrument of policy leverage' to influence Egyptian actions, which was unacceptable. 'If the United States is ready to sell me arms' said the President, 'I shall be very happy; I shall also be happy if the Soviet Union wishes to negotiate new sales.' Expressing strong confidence in the ultimate success of Dr Kissinger's peacemaking efforts, Mr Sadat paid a tribute to the US Secretary of State as 'a real strategist who has succeeded in revolutionising American policy in the Middle East'.

(from *Keesing's Contemporary Archives*, 1974)

Russia and other Arab States

To counterbalance her declining influence in Egypt, Russia has in recent years developed links with other Arab countries including Libya, Syria, Algeria and the Yemen. In this way Russia has been able to limit American influence in the Middle East. At the same time the Russians have also been able to exert influence over Arab countries supplying oil to European states, such as France, Britain and West Germany.

THE INVOLVEMENT OF THE USA

Until World War Two the United States of America was not deeply involved in the Middle East. US policy usually followed the lead of Great Britain. After 1945 the development of Russian activity and

A cartoon from an American newspaper of October 1973, commenting on the American attitude to the Middle East situation

"Don't worry, Abdul, with this disguise the Americans won't let them shoot!"

the decline of British power caused the United States to increase its own interest in the area.

The United States aimed to maintain friendly relations with all countries in the Middle East but this soon proved impossible. United States support for the United Nations partition plan for Palestine in 1947, immediate recognition of Israel in May 1948, and her **support of Israel's** application for member-

President Eisenhower

American tanks and supplies arriving in Lebanon, 1958

ship of the United Nations in 1949 antagonised the Arab states. In 1954, with US support, Iran, Turkey, Pakistan and Iraq signed the Baghdad Pact for mutual security and economic development. This agreement was strongly opposed by Russia, Egypt, Syria and Saudi Arabia. To counter this pact Egypt made an arms deal with Communist Czechoslovakia. The United States responded by refusing to approve Egypt's application for a loan from the World Bank where she had considerable power. The Suez War of 1956 resulted in the loss of much of Britain's influence and the growth of that of Russia.

The Eisenhower doctrine

The United States began to give diplomatic, military and economic assistance to non-Communist states in the Middle East—particularly to Israel and to those states which seemed likely to fall under Communist influence. This policy known as the Eisenhower Doctrine, was endorsed by the Congress of the United States in 1957 (Source 40).

A cartoon from a Cairo newspaper in May 1967: it depicts the Arab forces (giant armed figure, right) and US President Johnson who is hugging a shivering Israeli. Johnson is saying to the Arabs: "Have pity on him! Isn't his economic depression enough?'

In 1958 President Eisenhower sent American marines into the Lebanon in response to an appeal from the President who claimed that his country was in danger from Communist elements from inside and outside his borders. The independence of the Lebanon was secured and American troops were withdrawn by October 1958.

In the 1960s, the United States extended increasing economic aid and military supplies to Israel. This policy was designed to secure a foothold from which to counter Russian influence in the Middle East. It was partly a result of the strong campaign on behalf of Israel by the Jewish community in the United States. Unlike the western European countries America was not dependent on Arab states for oil supplies.

The principles of US policy in the Arab-Israeli dispute were summed up by President Johnson in June 1967 (Source 41). Three problems for the United States in relation to the Middle East were also broadly outlined. These included problems stemming from the American desire to have friendly relations with both Israel and the Arab states, the efforts of Russia to reduce American influence and to expand its own power in the area and the disturbing impact of western ideas and living standards on the developing Arab countries in the Middle East.

Source 40

THE EISENHOWER DOCTRINE, MARCH 9th 1957

Resolved, That the President be and hereby is authorised to cooperate with and assist any nation or group of nations in the general area of the Middle East desiring such assistance in the development of economic strength dedicated to the maintenance of national independence.

Sec. 2. The President is authorised to undertake, in the general area of the Middle East, military assistance programs with any nation or group of nations of that area desiring such assistance. Furthermore, the United States regards as vital to the national interest and world peace the preservation of the independence and integrity of the nations in the Middle East. To this end, if the President determines the necessity thereof, the United States is prepared to use armed force to assist any such nation or group of nations requesting assistance against armed aggression from any country controlled by international communism, provided that such employment shall be consonant with the treaty obligations of the United States and with the Constitution of the United States.

(from *Documents of American History*, Henry Steele Commager, Prentice-Hall, Inc., 1973)

"And the desert (provided certain guarantees are undertaken) shall rejoice (given a measure of mutual forbearance) and blossom (nationalism and age-old hatreds permitting) as the rose (always supposing an absence of outside interference)" — Isaiah. 35. 1.

A Punch *cartoon of August 1967, commenting on the essential preconditions for a settlement of the Arab-Israeli conflict*

PRESIDENT JOHNSON'S PRINCIPLES OF US POLICY 1967

1. Each nation in the area must have the right to live without threat of attack or extinction.

2. More than a million homeless Arab refugees must be settled justly before a lasting peace can be achieved.

3. Maritime rights must be respected; rights of innocent passage through international waterways must be preserved for all nations.

4. Arms shipments into the area should be reduced and limited on all sides, thus reducing tensions and freeing capital for vital economic development.

5. Secure and recognised territorial boundaries must be established in order to achieve respect for the political and territorial integrity of all states in the region.

(*Issues in United States Foreign Policy: The Middle East,* published by the Department of State, USA 1968)

BIOGRAPHY: DR HENRY KISSINGER

Dr Kissinger was born in Germany in 1923 and fled with his family from the Nazi persecution of the Jews in 1938 to the USA. He studied accountancy before serving in the army in World War II (1939–45). After the war, he went to Harvard University. On gaining his PhD he became a teacher there. By 1962 Dr Kissinger was a Professor of Government and had written two books which established him as a leading authority on US Strategic Policy. He acted as a consultant to the Government on security matters from 1955–1968.

In 1968, President Nixon appointed Dr Kissinger as assistant to the President for national security affairs. He quickly became far more influential in foreign policy than the Secretary of State, William Rodgers. He soon achieved world wide fame for his diplomatic activities. These included developing good relations between the United States and China, and negotiating the withdrawal of American troops from Vietnam. In 1972, he shared the Nobel Peace Prize with North Vietnamese negotiator Le Duc Tho for his part in securing a peace settlement. In 1973 Kissinger was appointed Secretary of State. He became so indispensable as the leading American diplomat that he survived the disgrace and resignation of President Nixon after the Watergate scandal.

After securing a cease-fire through the UN in the Yom Kippur War of 1973 Dr Kissinger tried hard to negotiate a permanent peace settlement in the Middle East. At this time he engaged in 'shuttle diplomacy', travelling from one Middle Eastern capital to another, without, it seemed, even allowing himself time to sleep. He established particularly friendly relations with President Anwar Sadat of Egypt. In January 1974 he succeeded in securing an Israeli-Egyptian Disengagement agreement on the Suez Front. In May 1974 of the same year, he negotiated a similar agreement between Israel and Syria on the Golan Front.

Kissinger has been trying to ensure the security and survival of Israel, without endangering European oil supplies by antagonising the Arabs. He continued his policy of negotiating a permanent peace in the Middle East through 1976 but without final success.

*Discussions in progress at the Geneva
Peace Conference, 1974*

PROSPECTS FOR THE FUTURE

The Middle East is only one area of the world which provides the setting for the rivalry of the super-powers. Nevertheless, it is one of the most dangerous. There can be no doubt that the great powers have contributed to the intensity of the conflict by failing to implement the arms embargo in the area to which they agreed in 1950.

US Secretary of State Henry Kissinger discussing terms for an interim peace agreement with Israeli leaders, January 1975

The October war in 1973 clearly revealed the dangers inherent in the policies of the super-powers. After the earlier war of 1967 both powers had resumed shipments of arms to their client states in the Middle East. During the war a confrontation between Russia and America seemed a real possibility. It appeared that Russia was preparing to send troops into the area. America at once declared a world-wide military alert. However, at that point, each power committed no further provocative acts and began to exert pressure on their allies to limit the scope and intensity of the conflict. Armistice negotiations and, later, a peace conference, took place.

Dr Kissinger meets President Sadat of Egypt during negotiations over the disengagement agreement in March 1975: this was Kissinger's fifth visit to Alexandria in ten days

The interim agreement between Israel and Egypt, signed in September 1975, was the result of Dr Kissinger's Middle East shuttle diplomacy and was heralded at the time as 'Pax Americana'. It seemed to point to the fact that the UN can never be a substitute for the super-powers in providing military guarantees, but it also pointed to a danger: that if one of the super-powers acted alone the other (in this case Russia) might feel aggrieved and be more inclined to join more directly with one side or group. It seems that any lasting peace in the Middle East must fulfil three conditions:

1. the Arab world must accept Israel's sovereignty;

2. there must be permanent frontier settlements which return to the Arabs most of the land occupied after the 1967 war;

3. a Palestinian State must be established to redress legitimate Palestinian grievances.

To be effective such an agreement would have to be guaranteed by the super-powers.

GLOSSARY

acquiesce—accept quietly

acquiescence—uncomplaining acceptance

administration—government

anarchy—disorder and confusion in a society where there is no government and where there are no laws to control people's actions

annexed—adjoining, attached

anti-semitism—hatred/feeling against the Jews

arduous—hard to do

aspirations—hopes, aims

assimilate—to absorb an alien group into the normal life of the majority of people in the country

assimilation—joining together and absorption of different groups into one nation

auspices—protective leadership

Barbary pirates—pirates from the north coast of Africa who used to terrorise sailors and loot ships in the Mediterranean Sea area

belligerency—war

boycott—refusal to buy or use something, often for political reasons

by virtue of—because of

Caliph—the civil and religious leader of all Muslims

client states—less powerful states dependent on the super-powers for military supplies and economic aid

coercion—forcible persuasion, compulsion

colonial—being ruled by another more powerful and usually more advanced state

concessions—rights over the Suez Canal and revenue income from it

concurrently—at the same time as

confederation—league or alliance

congealed—stopped flowing and solidified

contemplates—considers, thinks seriously about

creeds—religions

culminating—building up to a climax

degradation—disgrace

dehydration—lack of water

demilitarized zones—areas where no military forces, weapons or installations are allowed

deportation—compulsory expulsion from the country

derision—ridicule

dilemma—the problem of not being able to decide which of two equally unpleasant policies to follow

disenfranchisement—withdrawal of the citizens' voting rights

dislocation—being out of place

durable—lasting

economic integration—encouragement of the refugees to take jobs, set up businesses, and establish homes outside the camps, and so earn their own living and participate in the economy of the country like its other inhabitants

edifice—structure or building

endeavours—efforts

endorsed—formally approved of

enlightenment—instruction

enterprise—setting up and conducting business and trade

exonerating—finding someone not guilty of something

exploitation—making a profit yourself at the expense of others. President Nasser was referring to the money made by the Suez Canal Company in Egypt

facades—the outward appearances

facilitate—make easy

Fascist—extremely right wing, anti-democratic and nationalistic

fatalistic—feeling unable to do anything to prevent the worst happening, believing it to be inevitable

federated—a number of states joined together in a League

feign Islam—pretend to be acting in the name of all Muslims

feudalism—a system developed in Europe in the middle ages by which lesser nobles, or vassals, were granted land in exchange for fighting for their Lords-Superior when required. President Nasser was comparing the historical position of Egypt in relation to Britain and the rest of the Western World, to the position of a vassal in the middle ages who was bound to do as his Lord ordered

fiasco—a complete failure

friction—disagreement, bad relations

functionaries—officials

grandeur—greatness

holocaust—the mass murder of the Jews during World War II (1939–45)

impelled—driven on

imperialism—the economic and political control of weak and underdeveloped countries by more powerful developed countries

incompatible—cannot go together or co-exist at all

ingenuity—inventive skill and cunning

intimate—close

inviolability—sacred right to be protected from violence

irrepressible—impossible to put down

Jewry—the Jewish people all over the world

journals—parts of the axles of wheels

jurisdiction—legal authority

kibbutzim—communal farming centres where all the villagers cooperated in the farming of the land and the sale of its produce, and in performing many of the domestic and child rearing tasks normally carried out by individual families

Kosher butchery—killing of Jewish people in the same way that the Jewish religion lays down for the killing of animals for Kosher, or pure, meat

latent—hidden, existing but not yet developed

legitimate—lawful

liquidated—killed off

lyddite—a powerful explosive

mandated—placed under the rule of more advanced states by the League of Nations

mandatory—the state ruling the mandated territory

monopoly—the exclusive control or possession

of something. President Nasser was referring to the Anglo-French control of the Suez Canal

object—goal, aim

objectives—aims or goals

obligations—legal duties

oppression—unjust, tyrannical control

oppressive tyrant—a dictator who uses the absolute power he has over his subjects cruelly and harshly

paradox—something which conflicts with, or goes against what is reasonable or possible

parody—mocking imitation

perceptible—able to be seen and recognised easily by others

perpetuation—deliberate continuation, prolongation

potentialities—possibilities for development

precedent—previous examples or cases

preconceived—planned beforehand

prejudice—affect, impair

protectorate—a territory under the guardianship and rule of the government of another state

proverbial—so famous that you are held up as an example

Rabbis—Jewish religious leaders who are given the power to deal with questions of Jewish law and rituals

repatriation—returning people to live in their native land

sentiment—feeling or emotion

shechita—Jewish ritual slaughter of animals, according to which the animal is killed, without being stunned first, by the cutting of the carotid arteries and jugular vein immediately behind the jawbone

sovereign—legally independent and holding supreme power

sovereignty—the legal right to absolute authority and supreme power

spontaneous—natural and unforced

stringent—strict

surveillance—strict supervision, being watched very closely

suzerainty—rulership

synagogues—Jewish places of worship, the Jewish equivalent of Christian churches or Muslim mosques

territorial integrity—the right of a country to control all the land within its borders without fear of attack from another country

tenacious—tough, stubborn

The Jewish Agency—an organisation established in 1929 to secure the cooperation of all Jews, not just Zionists, to assist in the establishment of the Jewish national home. It was linked to the World Zionist Organisation

turmoil—upheaval and unrest

tyranny—cruel and harsh misgovernment by a dictator who has absolute power over his subjects

unassailable—cannot be contradicted or attacked

usurping—taking over rights belonging to others

vilayets—provinces forming part of the Turkish Empire, ruled by a *vali*, or governor-general

visas—a stamp or paper inserted into a passport, allowing entry into a country

World Bank—This was established in 1945, to help in the reconstruction and development of territories of member countries by encouraging investment of foreign money and arranging loans for them. Since the war, it has helped finance many large projects, such as dam building in developing countries. The United States has always been influential in deciding which countries should receive its assistance

ACKNOWLEDGEMENTS

The authors and publishers are grateful to the following for permission to reproduce copyright material:

Photographs and illustrations

page 4 *oil refinery in the Persian Gulf*, Camera Press;

page 5 *Jews and Arabs outside the Israeli Embassy*, Free Palestine Information Office, London;

page 6 *Egyptian attack, 1973*, Keystone Press Agency;

page 7 *opening ceremony, Suez Canal* and *French postcard*, Radio Times Hulton Picture Library;

page 8 *Punch* cartoon, *Disraeli and Suez*, reproduced by permission of *Punch*;

page 11 *attack on a Jew in Kiev*, Mansell Collection;

page 13 *Theodor Herzl*, Mansell Collection;

page 13 *Weizmann and Balfour*, Radio Times Hulton Picture Library;

page 15 *Sherif Hussein of Mecca*, Historical Picture Service;

page 16 *Sir Henry McMahon*, portrait by William Roberts, Jonathan Cape and the Lawrence Trustees;

page 17 *Feisal, son of Sherif Hussein*, Imperial War Museum, London;

page 18 *Lawrence of Arabia*, Imperial War Museum, London;

page 19 *wrecked railway trucks, Ghedir el Hej*, Imperial War Museum, London;

page 21 *Arthur James Balfour*, Mansell Collection;

page 24 *Jewish settlers*, Israeli Embassy;

page 25 *riots in Palestine*, Keystone Press Agency;

page 26 *demonstration in Jerusalem*, Israeli Embassy;

page 27 *Jewish refugees*, Keystone Press Agency;

page 27 *German SS men*, Weiner Library, London;

page 28 *inmates of a German concentration camp*, Imperial War Museum, London;

page 29 *King David Hotel*, Jerusalem, Israeli Embassy;

page 31 *David Ben-Gurion proclaims State of Israel*, Israeli Embassy;

page 32 *Knesset Building*, Israeli Embassy;

page 33 *European Jews*, Jewish National Fund;

page 34 *Rabbis reading the Law*, Radio Times Hulton Picture Library;

page 35 *Negev Desert* and *tree nursery*, Radio Times Hulton Picture Library;

page 36 *Kibbutz Sheluhot*, Israeli Embassy; *King Farouk*, Keystone Press Agency;

page 37 *President Nasser and others*, Keystone Press Agency;

page 38 *oil tanker passing through Suez Canal*, Radio Times Hulton Picture Library;

page 39 *Aswan High Dam*, Keystone Press Agency

page 40 *Anwar Sadat*, Keystone Press Agency;

page 41 *stamp*, courtesy of Stanley Gibbons;

page 45 *British newspapers, 1956*, Radio Times Hulton Picture Library;

page 46 *Israeli troops*, Radio Times Hulton Picture Library;

page 47 *Egyptian troops, Sharm el Sheikh*, and *Israeli army on manoeuvres*, Popperfoto; *watch tower*, Israeli Embassy;

page 48 *General Dayan*, Keystone Press Agency; *detachment of Israeli army*, Popperfoto;

page 49 *Moshe Dayan*, Israeli Embassy; *Punch* cartoon, reproduced by permission of *Punch*;

page 50 *Golda Meir*, Keystone Press Agency;

page 52 *King Hussein of Jordan* and *Russian SAM missile*, Keystone Press Agency;

page 53 *wreckage of Syrian army vehicles*, Popperfoto;

page 56 *the Wailing Wall*, Jerusalem, Radio Times Hulton Picture Library;

page 57 *stamp*, courtesy of Stanley Gibbons; *Mosque of Omar*, Jerusalem, Popperfoto;

page 58 *Cairo demonstration*, Popperfoto; *heading from* L'Express, L'Express, Paris;

page 59 *school*, Israeli Embassy;

page 60 *Arab quarter, Jerusalem*, Radio Times Hulton Picture Library;

page 61 *stamp*, courtesy of Stanley Gibbons;

page 62 *refugee camp, East Jordan*, United Nations Relief and Works Agency;

page 63 *refugee camp, Syria*, United Nations, UNRWA;

page 64 *camp near Amman, Jordan*, United Nations, UNRWA;

page 66 *Abba Eban*, Keystone Press Agency;

page 68 *Palestine guerrillas*, Keystone Press Agency;

page 70 *refugees*, Popperfoto;

page 71 *Yasser Arafat*, Popperfoto;

page 72 *wreckage of aircraft*, Keystone Press Agency; *Jewish children*, Israeli Embassy;

page 73 *Nasser and others*, Keystone Press Agency;

page 74 *UN headquarters, New York*, Keystone Press Agency;

page 75 *stamp*, courtesy of Stanley Gibbons; *refugee camp*, Israeli Embassy;

page 76 *refugee camp*, United Nations, UNRWA;

page 77 *UN troops*, Popperfoto;

page 78 *Kissinger and Waldheim* and *Nasser and U Thant*, Keystone Press Agency;

page 79 *Israeli troops*, Popperfoto;

page 80 *Arafat at the UN*, United Nations;

page 81 *cartoon*, by permission of *Punch*;
page 82 *Israeli forces* and *Russian warship*,
Popperfoto;
page 84 *Kissinger and Sadat*, Popperfoto;
page 85 *cartoon*, *Philadelphia Daily News*
Oct. 1973;
page 86 *President Eisenhower* and *American
troops*, Keystone Press Agency;
page 87 *cartoon*, Popperfoto;
page 88 *cartoon*, by permission of *Punch*;
page 89 *Dr Henry Kissinger*, Keystone Press
Agency;
page 90 *Kissinger with Israeli Leaders*, Popperfoto;
page 91 *Kissinger with Sadat*, Popperfoto;

The authors and publishers have made every
effort to trace copyright owners of material used
in this book. In cases where they have been
unsuccessful they apologise for any accidental
infringement of copyright.

Extracts
Source 1 S. Haim, *Arab Nationalism; An
Anthology*, © 1962 by Regents of the University
of California, reprinted by permission of the
University of California Press;
Sources 2,3,6,8,10-12,14,18,20,29,34 Walter
Laqueur (ed), *The Israel Arab Reader*, Weidenfeld
& Nicolson Ltd, 1969;
Source 7 T. E. Lawrence, *Seven Pillars of
Wisdom*, Jonathan Cape Ltd and the Seven
Pillars Trust;
Source 15 *The Jerusalem Post*, Jerusalem, Israel;
Source 4 reproduced by permission of
Sir Richard Sykes;
Source 5 Crown copyright, reproduced by
permission of Her Majesty's Stationery Office;
Source 21 Noble Frankland (ed), *Documents of
International Affairs, 1956*, by permission of the
Oxford University Press;
Source 23 reproduced by permission of *The
Israeli Economist*, Jerusalem, Israel;
Source 25 by permission of the League of Arab
States Office, London;
Source 31, 36 by permission of *Free Palestine*,
London;
Source 32 by permission of *The Daily
Telegraph;*
Source 37 reproduced from W. Schramm,
One Day in the World's Press, Stanford
University Press, 1969, by permission of
Stanford University Press, Stanford, California;
Source 40 Henry Steele Commager (ed),
Documents of American History, 9th ed. © 1973.
Reprinted by permission of Prentice-Hall Inc.,
Englewood Cliffs, New Jersey;
Source 41 by permission of the United States
Information Service.